Not Quite Love

Ryan Onstad

All the names have been changed to protect people's privacy as well as some elements of personal information, composites and attributes. The events that take place are my recollection to the best of my knowledge of them. However, the stories you are about to read, as well as my name, are all true.

Dedicated to my mother, may you always be proud of me.

To the dreamers:

May this book be an inspiration to you, for the simple fact that it's proof, no matter how good or bad this book may be, that if you put your mind to it, you can do anything! No matter people's reaction, for better or worse, you too can find a way to accomplish what you feel led to do. Don't let anything or anyone stand in your way!

Prologue: This Is Who I Am

To understand why the following stories you are about to read are semi-tragic, you have to understand the person they affected most… me.

I'm just like many of you. I'm everyone, yet no one. I'm a unique individual. My background and life story are similar to some of you, yet uniquely different from others.

For a lack of better terms, if I'm going to be the "hero" of this story, then let me tell you about myself, so you can have someone to root for.

Allow me to introduce myself: my name is Ryan.

Life got started right off the bat unlike anyone in my family tree I came to find out… I was adopted. Born in Omaha, NE and shipped to Lincoln, NE three days later (a little adoption joke some laugh at). My birth father was a traveling musician and my birth mom used to work for the F.B.I., doing paperwork; she wasn't an agent like Dana Scully from *The X-Files*, one of my favorite shows of all time, but I digress.

I was adopted into a loving family, my mother was a former elementary school teacher and my father has his P.H.D. in mathematics and became a computer analyst. Eventually, my dad got into computer coding and made a living teaching old computers to talk to new computers… however, it didn't pay "Apple" money, that's for sure!

I grew up in a normal white-picket-fence world, went to good schools, had good friends and had it a lot better than others for many reasons. My parents never beat me or did drugs. They always provided for me; I was an only child, so I was the only thing they really had to focus on!

Despite my presence in their life, my dad faded out in my life fast. Sure, he made the money and put the food on the table, but other than that, he checked out emotionally. My dad was never one who wanted to go on those father/son fishing trips, etc. and by my teen years and still today, we don't really talk much. Deep inside I know my father loves me; he just has a hard time expressing it. My mother assumed the role of lead parent early on. Since she was a school teacher, it was in her blood, I suppose.

My parents taught me that love is about commitment, that despite the fact that some people grow apart, there is still a foundation that brings them together. They are committed to making things work, which few couples can say today. Instead of quitting, they choose to try to find new and different ways to communicate and grow together.

As the saying goes, "A ring don't mean nothing if you can't hold the weight." Well, they certainly have carried theirs like Frodo headed to Mordor!

In elementary school, I was the man! I played every sport imaginable, minus football. My mother banned me from it because she was afraid that I would injure myself. I was also the tallest kid in school for the longest time, so I was often guaranteed a starting position and didn't have to be really that good! Sports was my life for a long time. Summers on the baseball field with a mouthful of nice and salty sunflower seeds… nothing better than that, I thought!

In my off time from my various athletic fields, my escape was music. I loved listening to anything with rhythm and groove, I was drawn to anything that was untypical and not simple composition wise, not poppy and bubble gum like; needless to say, my musical tastes gravitated toward metal.

By this time, my parent's health started to get bad. My mother is a cancer survivor. On top of that, by this time in life, she had already been in 11 car accidents, none were her fault, from stupid teenagers, drunk drivers; they all seemed to find her on the road. I was in 3 of the accidents with her. She was either really lucky or really cursed, depending on how you look at it! Either way, my mom would spend many days on the floor, not even enough strength to make it into her own bed… so I helped take care of her a lot of times.

My father's health didn't fare much better either… over the years, he has had cancer twice and suffers from Crohn's disease, so what manly duties he couldn't do around the house, I had to lend a hand in his place.

In the 6th grade, life took a dive for me. My asthma for some reason got bad… my lungs weren't growing as fast as my body and subsequently, athletics were cut out... except baseball; if I didn't have that, I don't know what I would have done!

Middle school came and my health took another hit. I developed a digestive deficiency that was hard to originally diagnose. This resulted in me having severe stomach pains. They were crippling at times. I'd be fine one second and then hunched over on the floor the next. This issue was eventually resolved when the doctors found out my body didn't produce some protein and certain enzymes, but for a year, it was a living hell!

The rest of middle school was a blur; without my athletic friends, I had virtually no one, less than three friends to my name. Two of those at this point also got into drugs and since I wasn't into that stuff, the calls to hang out were few and far between.

Still to this day, I've never had a sip of alcohol nor done a single drug. Though neither "straight edge" nor a legalist, it was a choice I made for myself about this time in my life, that I wouldn't do those things, because addiction was something that was present in my biological family.

I also grew to have severe back and neck issues too. I got teased a lot, no thanks to the back brace that looked more like a bra! If I had one that was just a giant metal pipe, I might have faired better!

I spent many days alone, just me and my music. My friends were Van Halen, Def Leppard, Extreme, Aerosmith. If it rocked, I listened to it. By this time as well, I had taken up the drums and fell in love with them!

During my final year of Middle School, I received a final hit to my health that almost did me in. I contracted a severe case of mono. I missed nearly 2/3rds of the school year. I was a virtual ghost. No friends. I lived for one thing at that point, Saturday night... my ritual was watching "Saturday Night Live" then "Headbanger's Ball".

My friends now were the cast of SNL and Anthrax, Pantera, Metallica and Dream Theater.

When I arrived at high school, no one recognized me. I wore glasses now. I didn't go to school-sponsored games or school functions. I avoided them to dodge being teased. I still had baseball in the summer, but what teammates I had, didn't think much of me, no matter how well I did on the field because off the field, I was a square. That in part is why I didn't get invited to parties or was able to be friends with the people I so desperately wanted to have accept me.

I wanted to die. I had a plan. It would have worked too.

Then things changed.

When I was in the 2nd grade, I accepted Christ as my personal savior… now beyond that, it was meaningless. It was merely "Hell insurance." I'd pray here and there, but when nothing good came in life and in fact when it just kept getting worse, God and I were not friends.

So by the summer heading into my junior year, I stopped praying. I cursed God and told him that if he really had a better way for me, than lets see it, otherwise, I didn't care to talk to him; I cussed him out, re-plotted my quickest and easiest course of death and was ready to clock out.

A few weeks after that day, I met my youth pastor through a bunch of circumstances that showed it was clear; God was making our paths cross. Long story short, I finally understood who Jesus was and what he meant to my life. Through my youth group, I met the majority of my friends who are my closest companions today and have been for nearly twenty years.

I finally caught a break. I had God, my friends and now music. I joined my first band! I taught myself how to play bass by watching videos of Steve Harris of Iron Maiden play and ironically enough, helped start the worship band in my church's youth group.

The church band led to my first real band, which made my senior year of High School a blur. I went to school, got good grades and then immediately was allowed to play my bass. I also got a part time job at a local radio station as a DJ. At school I was a zero; outside of it, I was a rock star in training.

When college came, when everyone was out getting drunk and laid, I was showing up to class, getting grades and then immediately off to do band things. I had no time for distractions.

Eventually, the band started to go somewhere. Enough so I was able to convince my parents that dropping out of college was the best option. We recorded a demo, got airplay, touring offers and a real management company interested in us. But we eventually broke up and with none of the success I had hoped for. My bandmates and friends all were getting married at this point and I was getting left behind.

I got a job in medical records at a local hospital, and I still had my radio DJ gig, but with my parents continued failing health and them letting me build a recording studio in their basement, I remained at home.

I joined a few more bands as the years went by, but none achieved the success of the first. But, it didn't stop me from treating them like my "wife." I poured everything I had into them, financially and creatively. I figured the women and fortune would just follow after all my hard work paid off.

However, it wasn't like I didn't try. I just didn't have the cool moves, the catchy things to grab women's attention, frankly I was plain. What few took interest, were quickly turned off when they realized I had morals. Seriously, in my experience, say you believe in Jesus and they run in the other direction!

After the band life, a part of me died.

My friends were all now married with kids and solid jobs and structured lives; mine wasn't.

I spend a lot of my free time helping others, but just not myself. I went on missions trips to foreign countries on a regular basis. I did secular relief work as well. I lived to serve others and show Christ's love through my actions.

However, inside I was falling apart and was about to implode.

Eventually, I fell into depression and suicidal thoughts again, except, I found a new coping mechanism; instead of being stereotypical like the rock stars before me with alcohol and drugs, I found food.

No joke, at my worst, I was eating 6-8,000 calories a day. My nutritionist and I did the math: one day, I almost hit 9,000 calories! I was out of control. A standard meal would be an XL "works" pizza from Papa Johns. If I was in a rush, 2 foot long subs with extra meat and cheese at Subway. The worst was two burritos from Chipotle. Sometimes I would do that twice a day with a large buttered popcorn at the movies and a giant soda to boot. I was an eating machine. Once I even ate three Chipotle burritos in thirty minutes; the manager took pity on me and gave me a free shirt, which should have doubled as a bib for my fat ass! I was spending over $400 a month just on fast food!

My existence then became eating, video games and movies. When I wasn't at home watching endless hours of TV and video games, I was at the theatre.

I didn't fit in much anywhere. I was depressed, lonely and pathetic and that was even with God in my life.

Eventually, my doctor did some routine blood work and told me that I had less than two years to live or I would be dead of a heart attack, just like my biological father, who died at 32 (the same age as me at the time of this news) of a massive heart attack.

After a heartfelt plea from my best friend, I cleaned up my act the next day.

I got a gym membership, a nutritionist and threw all the junk food and soda away. I ate 2,000 calories a day, ate a regular diet: 3 meals a day.

In the first two weeks, no exercise, just changing my diet, I lost 24 pounds!

Add exercising six days a week and I lost 95 pounds in nine months! My doctor wanted 50 pounds gone in a year's span, I also most doubled that and I tried actually, until my doctor cut me off.

Once I lost the weight, then the girls gave me the time of day… it only took 34 years!

These are the events that shaped me to become the man that I am now. My life has been about overcoming negative circumstances and pushing forward and finding happiness and joy in them.

But everything I experienced showed me how to do things different should the opportunity ever come in my own life. If I do get married, I will never go to bed angry with my wife, no matter how big or small the issue might be. I will be ready to eat crow whenever it's called for. If I become a parent, I will teach them through grace how this world works. I will be the constant ear as to their needs. No matter how much they may begrudge it in their teenage years, I will always make sure to have time set aside for our family to do things together, despite our collective busy schedules.

I'm creative, fun and funny. Brutally honest and loyal to a fault! One of the few to still have a moral compass and follow it without faltering too hard. I don't have all the answers in this world, nor do I claim to. I love my family, friends and The Lord. I live to serve others and have with my time, via my volunteer work locally and through my missions work.

Now, if I could just find someone who wants to team up with me!

I've had an online dating profile for almost 15 years, it's been viewed nearly 5,000 times over the years. That's roughly 333 women who check me out each year, or 28 women a month who consider me.

If she is still out there, when I find her I hope that every time I see her, I can't wait to hear her speak, find comfort in her voice and eagerly anticipate what thing is daily happening in her life that'll keep me on my toes. I hope she is passionate about helping others, just as I am. If we're building something together, I'll hold the boards and she'll hit the nails! But most of all, I can't wait to have a companion, someone who is funny in her own way, just as I am in mine. Finally, someone who isn't ready to bail at the first sign of trouble, but instead, willing to working through the difficulties of life with love and grace.

So, until Katy Perry calls… the search continues!

Chapter 1
Hold Me, Thrill Me, Kiss Me, Kill Me

Annia Taylor—how was I to know this name would inflict such deep emotional pain? It all started innocently enough…

We first met on an online dating website. I would tell you which one, but it's name is something that is used to start a fire. And a fire is exactly what started in my heart when I first laid eyes on Annia's profile.

From the moment I first saw her picture, I knew she was something special. She was gorgeous. She had the most seductive eyes. She reminded me of Alexandra Breckenridge, who played a witch on *American Horror Story*, right down to the hooked witch's nose. And once I got to know Annia, I realized it was a perfect comparison, in the most flattering way possible. But regardless, her nose didn't matter to me; it wasn't long before she was my one in a million--perfect in my eyes.

Her profile immediately stuck out to me: she had a sense of humor and was clearly creative; she was into horror films, and, most importantly, had a firm Christian foundation for her beliefs. She came across like the type of gal that could talk about the Bible in a non-judgmental, non-legalistic way while holding a beer in the other hand. And I would soon learn I was right.

I mustered the courage to message her. I gave her a few paragraphs of compliments and she responded. This was a step up for me, because most women wouldn't even bother to respond with a polite rejection, let alone something positive. When she wrote back, she complimented some things about me that people often miss and so I knew then and there that this might actually go somewhere.

We started chatting online through the dating website for a week as well as regularly corresponding over email and then without warning, she disappeared.

"What happened?" I wondered. We talk every day for a week, and then suddenly nothing. I tracked her down on Facebook, and was stunned at her confession. She told me that she canceled her subscription because she decided to get back together with her ex-boyfriend and wanted to give it a chance again and not lead other men on, including myself, but she didn't know how to say that to me… so she just bailed.

So I wrote back and told her, that should things not work out, please contact me, that I really wanted to know her, what she shared so far was awesome and that I would hate to miss out on a chance with her.

Over the next 8 weeks, life went on with my daily routine. But I missed her. Not because she was my only prospect and had actually responded to my message… but because there was something real in her words, something that drew me to her. I knew she was the only person who I really wanted to talk to. I just knew that she had the potential to be my best friend, my romantic partner, my everything!

8 weeks after she disappeared, I messaged her on Facebook.

> 🖂 Are you still seeing that guy? If so, I wish you the best of luck! But if not, I still think you're incredible and I'd love to get together with you again.

She responded fairly quickly, and I was thrilled with her response.

> 🖂 It totally bombed! We went out like twice, and all I can think about is messaging you!

So two days after my 34th birthday, I got the ultimate belated present: I got to go on a date with this amazing woman.

She lived an hour away, so after making the trek, we met at a local hipster bar, just blocks from where she lived. She showed up in a cool orange and black dress that she found at a thrift store—she told me Halloween was her favorite holiday, and I thought I had to be in heaven because that is my favorite holiday too. For the next 90 minutes, the conversation didn't stop. We shared ideas and thoughts on topical stuff. They say to not talk about politics or religion on a first date, but we tackled those in spades; it was like we were dying to know everything about each other, as if we wanted to find a flaw in one another somehow. She was a bit more liberal than me on some things, but I didn't care; I thought it was what made her unique.

We were so busy talking, we didn't even do introductions, and I didn't realize until later that I was pronouncing her name wrong the whole time. I thought it was just a unique spelling of "Anna," but it's actually pronounced "Ah-nay-ah." Supposedly it means "priceless one" and was taken from a Roman Empress.

We saw eye to eye or at least fairly similarly on so many things, but one that set me at ease at the time was swearing. I had already told her that I lived with my parents (which was usually enough to send most women running) and eventually we got to talking about our vices. I admitted that I was embarrassed that I still struggled with swearing even though I had been a Christian for a long time. She grinned, cursed colorfully, and said, "It's your heart and your intent that matters!" I could have kissed her right there.

She was all kinds of dangerous too, and it didn't take long for me to see that she had lived a more worldly life than me. She bluntly told me about her past, that she used to frequent strip clubs and that she had been a lesbian for a few years. Although it was more than I expected, I didn't care; it merely made her more interesting and her current faith in Christ more real. "That was my old life," she said with a smile. "My new life is much more dull."

But she was anything but dull . She worked three jobs: she worked for the church she attended full time, a barista part time and then seasonally ran a Halloween themed business. Conversations with her were always interesting because she constantly had her hands in something new and exciting. I couldn't get enough; sometimes it was even hard to keep up or keep track of all the people she knew.

At some point, as I was listening to her crazy stories and antidotes of pure gold, I realized that I felt an incredibly deep connection to her. Then I felt a strange calm come over me—I've felt this one other time in my life, and the only thing I can attribute it to is the Holy Spirit—and I felt convicted that for some reason, God was asking me to honor her and protect her. Little did I know, that in the coming weeks, I would come to find out what that really meant.

After 90 minutes into the date, I thought things were going well, but I had never had a real date before, so it was tough to decide. Was this really happening or was this pretend? She told me her new roommate was going to be dropping by, that she met her over the internet and she just moved in with her 5 days before and had yet to actually talk to her. So her roommate dropped by and joined the fun. Now being a pessimist, I thought she was about to find an excuse to leave. Plus, this was double the pressure now; not only did I have to worry about impressing one girl but now two! But apparently I did all right—we spent the next two hours talking about anything and everything. But she was bonding with her new roommate too, so I eventually started to feel like wallpaper.

At the end of the night, I said goodbye, wondering what my final score had been. I couldn't tell if she liked me or not. She laughed a lot, smiled and nodded at many of my opinions and views… but who knows?

Maybe she was just being polite.

The next morning, I was still kind of confused. I didn't know what to think. Did she like me or not? I texted my friends' wives for advice.

> 🖂 Do I text her? Do I call her? It was so amazing…I don't want to screw this up!

My buddy Paul's wife Melissa texted me back immediately.

> 🖂 DO NOT TEXT HER! Whatever you do, don't say anything for two days to her. Otherwise she will think you are desperate.

I frustratingly responded back.

> 🖂 WTF??? That sucks!

My best friend Keith's wife Sarah chimed in at this point.

> 🖂 Yeah, it's the two day rule. And it's just part of the dating game. Get used to it.

I was mad! I thought she was the coolest person on the planet! I couldn't wait to talk to her again! Now I had to wait two whole days?

TWO WHOLE DAYS?

I looked at my phone and tried to resist texting her. I kept impatiently stuffing my face with Cheerios, when all of a sudden, *she* texted *me*!

> 🖂 Hey! I just wanted you to know I had a ton of fun last night! You are funny, smart and above all that, kind. I know you drove an hour to see just me, but you made my roommate feel welcome and that speaks highly of the person you are! ☺

And my brilliant response?

> 🖂 So… is this your way of telling me that you are going to let me take you out again?

She wrote back two simple words:

> 🖂 Well, duh!

And we were off and rolling.

From that point on, we texted each other practically every five minutes. Wherever I was, she was with me, maybe not physically, but electronically or in my mind. Finally, I found someone who I could share my thoughts and opinions with, and she didn't think I was insane.

She lived an hour away, so we had to be really intentional with our words and time, since she worked three jobs as well. But since it was my first real relationship, I didn't mind at all. If we lived in the same town, I might have suffocated her. Again, I had nothing but time on my hands and she had hardly any. So in essence, I felt lucky that I was the guy she chose to spend that free time with.

Before our second date, we had this long conversation one night. She hated talking on the phone for some reason, so I had to type or text like a fiend (which drove me nuts). She started getting deeper into her past and her life before she "got into God" and she told me that she had a secret that she has been freed from through Christ, but it was a turn off for a lot of guys. She didn't think it would be a big deal to me, but thought I should know. She went on to tell me a pretty awful and torrid story of being molested and raped over the years by several family members, neighbors, ex-boyfriends, religious figures and men who took advantage of her during alcohol-infused encounters. Sexual abuse was rampant in her life. Nearly every male figure in her life had sexual contact with her at some point it seemed.

Beyond that, her mother was nothing short of a monster. She physically abused Annia to the point that Annia and her brother were removed from the home. And to add to that, he was killed a few years before we met in a car accident.

Simply put, tragedy followed her.

I didn't pity her. I only wanted to love on her more and be by her side to process more of those thoughts and feelings. I was fine with just listening. I thought of the feelings I'd had on our first date, and my desire to honor and protect her grew and grew.

After opening up about her past, she explained how that affected her relationships.

> 🖂 So…because of all that, I have a REALLY hard time expressing my feelings.

My heart broke a little for her, but my response set her at ease:

> 🖂 I have no problem sharing my feelings with you. I think you are the coolest person on the planet! And because every guy has treated you so poorly, I will show you the exact opposite!

She simply replied:

> 🖂 ☺

I continued:

> 🖂 I will never try to kiss you or hold your hand until you have given me permission to do so. Until that point, I will just be the best companion you have ever had!

From that point on, that was our relationship: really getting to know each other on a deep, personal level without having to worry about expressing ourselves physically in order to keep the other around… but let's not kid ourselves. I was 34 and really looking forward to actually kissing a girl. And I finally had found the perfect one.

I went all out for her. Before our third date, one of her customers at the coffee shop brought her a purple rose… and I had yet to get her any flowers. So it was time to stake my claim. From that point on, I brought flowers to every date. That's twice a week, mind you. At least she hated roses, so I saved some money.

Beyond that, I had epic surprises for her.

One day on a road trip, my best friend Shaun and I went to a wine store to "buy our women wine." He has been married for nearly a decade (I was best man at his wedding) and has watched me get rejected over and over by women; he was around when Annia would text me, so he knew she was real. He was excited to meet this girl that finally liked me. And we were both jazzed for a potential double date; in high school and college, we had done everything together except that. And now we had an opportunity to take our women out together.

I ended up buying this fancy German wine that had a monkey etched into the bottle. Annia and I would later jokingly call it "Monkey Wine" because neither of us knew how to pronounce the actual name.

When the monkey wine was a hit, I surprised her two weeks later at work with every type and variation of Monkey Wine available on the market, plus flowers (which was all to the tune of nearly $300). I was going for the "companion of the year award" for sure!

Needless to say, I blew her out of the water (she may have been a little shell-shocked).

Another time, I dropped by unannounced after I was in town for a concert and left her 2 dozen cookies from a high-end local bakery and flowers for her to stumble over as she walked in the door after getting home from her second job. Plus, she was leaving out of town for a work retreat the next morning. I made sure she had plenty of cookies to share with everyone, with my name attached, letting her co-workers know I was her guy. Of course, this wasn't the best gift; she was a practicing Vegan and some of the ingredients in the cookies weren't Vegan friendly, so she didn't actually eat any of them, but she told me later it was the thought that counted.

I remember that next night—we texted while she lay in her hotel room after a long day of meetings about how she felt bad because she didn't know how to reciprocate the affection I showed her. And over and over I told her that I just wanted to love on her and when the time was right, she would know what to do for me.

It was in this same conversation that she told me for the first time about Chris. He was an ex-boyfriend, and she had gone to lunch with him the previous day. My body froze. He pleaded with her to come back to him, laying it out like a lawyer. I held my breath.

> 🖂 Don't worry, I told him you and I are together now.

I exhaled.

✉ You have nothing to worry about.

I felt myself relax. Of course I didn't need to worry. We texted every five minutes. We were electronically connected at the hip!

A few days later, she had a two-hour window in-between jobs and asked me to coffee. So on a Sunday morning, I drove up there and we just sipped drinks and talked. Everything was beautiful—the weather was quiet and peaceful, and I was falling in love. Her hair flowed in the light breeze, jet black with new, bright red highlights.

That morning, she started to reciprocate. She gave me a card with a dog on the front holding a bouquet of flowers and inside she wrote all the things she liked about me. That card, though maybe a small thing to most, was big to me. It was obvious that she had taken a lot of time and effort, and for the first time in my life, a woman wanted to get it on paper how meaningful I was to her.

A few weeks later, I had the ultimate surprise for her: a scavenger hunt. I bought her some earrings and a massage. She followed the map I made and was blown away when we made it to the massage parlor. I waited outside for an hour while she got loosened up. Then the plan was that I was going to take her back to her place, hide the earrings on this earring rack that she had in her room, and make her follow clues in order to discover them later in the evening.

But first, we stopped into a local pub where she got a beer and we just sat and talked theology. It was just a great night. It only got better when she let it slip that she had been invited to a friend's birthday party, but was skipping it to spend time exclusively with me. I was flattered, but told her that she shouldn't miss it because of our date and that I didn't mind stopping in and hobnobbing.

So we went to the party. And that was the first time that I should have seen the writing on the wall. Something was off.

When we got there, I saw only a few faces I recognized. Annia immediately left me and made a beeline to her girlfriend Cindy, who I hadn't met but had heard a lot about. Cindy had sort of an odd expression on her face as she looked at me, and I overheard Annia whisper, "He doesn't know..." I only caught part of it as I caught up with her, and I felt a little giddy as I wondered if this might be some continuation from her card the day before. It didn't really make sense at the time, and after the party, I took her home and headed back to Lincoln. And the comment slipped from my mind.

A few days later was October 15. I remember it well, because it was the day after my mother's birthday.

The night before had been a typical Monday. I was at my men's Bible study; she was at a bar watching Monday Night Football with her friends. We had texted back and forth whenever we could. But later, when we both were free, we were talking about her day and she only said that she didn't really want to talk about it. I, of course, knew this was girl-code for "I really want to talk about it, but you need to ask me."

After twenty minutes of trying to coax it out of her, she admitted that Chris, the ex, had been at the bar. I was immediately angry.

I snapped:

> ✉ What the hell was Chris doing there? I thought you made things clear with him!

She replied:

> ✉ My friends invited him. I didn't know.

I quickly replied, needing to know more obviously.

> ✉ Okay...so then what?

> ✉ Well...he saw me texting you and got pissed.

There was a long pause.

> ✉ He smashed my phone.

I couldn't believe it. But what came next was even harder to believe.

> ✉ So then, me and Ginger rode home together and she told Chris he could come with us.

Stunned I replied:

✉ Um. What?

She tried to calm the conversation down:

✉ It was no big deal. He calmed down and it was fine.

I knew I had to ask.

✉ Did you kiss him? Did he try to kiss you?

She quickly fired back with a reaffirming response.

✉ No!!!! I told him we were thru, remember?

I felt my blood pressure go back to normal, and my worry level started to decrease.

✉ Are you okay then?

Her response told me all I needed to know.

✉ Yeah. I am fine. He is sooooooo annoying!

In spite of the fact that I was relieved, it still really bothered me that Chris was hanging out with Annia and I was not. I was concerned.

So, fast forward to the next day, October 15th, the best and worst day of my life.

Our life plan at that time together was that on Wednesday the 16th, she and I were going out. We were going to get dressed up (which neither of us hardly ever did) and then I was going to take her to a play. Those seats were not cheap—together, they were close to $300. But I was going to go all out. It's Annia. How could I not? She was the one I loved. Then that weekend, Keith and Shaun (my two best friends) were going to visit her Halloween business with me, get a full tour of the place and then we'd take her to a movie and dinner. Keith and Shaun are like my family, so they were excited to finally meet her.

I canceled all my night plans for the 15th and headed straight to see her. I told her we needed to talk. I showed up in jeans, an old flannel shirt and a week-old beard; I looked fairly un-kept, but I was in a rush and was concerned about this Chris confrontation from the night before and I needed answers.

She admitted that originally, she had been afraid to tell me about being around Chris, so I brought her flowers to let her know I wasn't mad, but instead was attracted to her honesty. Because lets face it, ex-boyfriend's happen. They come and go out of people's lives. You have to adjust to their presence. Plus, they met up for lunch a few weeks back and she told him she was with me, so that took care of it. Or at least I thought it did.

So she and I sat down and talked. She said Chris was a jerk like he always apparently was in their relationship—he got drunk, smashed her phone. I believed her and I told her that when you drink and hang with ex's, nothing good usually happens and this event was a bi-product of that. She agreed that she needed to put her foot down and tell her friends to not invite him when she was around, and that it was disrespectful to me, the guy she is committed to.

We sat on her couch and kept talking. It then just turned into another night together. We were sipping on some tea she made, and I was helping her with her homework as she was just starting school to become a minister. It was a great night. To me, it was "bonus date night."

As the night progressed, she brought up a topic that we addressed earlier in our relationship and had actually talked about the week before in detail. And that was sex. I'm a virgin, she was not... several times over. She had sexual encounters with a lot of men and women. To be honest, I was fairly intimidated by her sexual experience.

"If we get married," I said, "by that point, God will help us work things out." She nodded. "Sex is all about communication. I believe that if we commit to being honest, and trust that God will do the rest to make our relationship work..." I added, "Well—I think it will be like riding a bike. Eventually I'll get better at it!" I grinned, and she smirked.

"Well," she said, "even though I'm a Christian, I don't believe that I have to wait to have sex till I'm married. But because that's what you want for us, out of respect to you, I will wait." I was frustrated that we did not share the same beliefs on that issue, but she trusted that I was in tune with what God wanted for us in a relationship and she trusted that, the answer she gave was good enough.

We also talked about the fact that we wanted to have children and that because of a complicated medical history, that bearing a child would be an issue too. But I told her, when we reach that point, again, God will provide. We also talked about wanting to adopt, since we were both adopted.

Pretty heavy stuff for a couple that hasn't even kissed, right?

She just kept smiling at my confidence in the fact that I knew she was the girl of my dreams and that God would take care of us and already had, by bringing us together.

Then I looked her in the eyes and said, "You mean everything to me. You are the first person I think of when I wake and the last before I sleep…"

Before I even finished my sentence, she leapt from the other end of the couch and started kissing me.

TOUCHDOWN!

After 34 for years of life, I finally kissed a girl, but not just anyone, "the one".

After she pulled away, I smiled and so did she and I said, "Did I do that right?"

She started laughing and said, "Oh yes, you are a very good kisser!" So I quickly responded with

"Then kiss me again!" She ran her fingers through my hair and her lips were pure ecstasy.

Then her damn roommate walked in the door.

Just as I was about to have potentially my first full-on make out session, her roommate arrived home and butted in as she always did. She talked our ears off about nonsense. I kept dropping hints for her to leave, go to her room and do this that and the other, but she wasn't catching my drift.

While Annia and her roommate were talking, I sneaked in a text to Sarah (she is the wife of Keith, one of my two best friends and Sarah is one of my closest female friends). I told her I just kissed Annia and details were to follow and she was beyond ecstatic.

Finally, the roommate had gone to her room and I said to Annia "So you bypassed the 'hand holding phase' entirely and went for kissing instead. Thanks. But I'd really like to hold your hand now." And so I did and we continued to talk the night away.

I asked her "Why did you decide to kiss me now?" She then smirked "I've thought about doing it for weeks now, but I didn't find the right way to act on it" I quickly responded, "You should have! Think of all the kisses we've missed out on since!"

As the night wore down, she walked me to my car and kissed me goodbye, with an even longer and deeper kiss than before. I ran my fingers through her hair, I touched the small of her back, we embraced each other in a long hug. I whispered in her ear, "I'm glad I waited all this time for you." She kissed me more and said softly, "I'm so blessed to have you".

As I drove home, I got no more than eight blocks away as I let out a loud "Yeah!" I was cheering in the privacy of my car, like I had just won the Super Bowl! This was a victory on all levels. I kissed the girl I was in love with, then I did the natural thing… I posted to the world of Facebook in a subliminal way. As I was driving home, she texted me as she was laying in bed and told me that she loved me.

> 🖂 I saw your Facebook post. I can't believe you think I'm your dream come true? How has no girl before me scooped you up? How could someone just only like you up till now and not love you? I'm falling in love with you. I can't wait to see you again tomorrow. You're my dream come true!

Life was complete.

As I got home, I ran straight to my computer and emailed my closest guy friends about this magical night. The thing was, my close guy friends are all married and since this was my first real relationship, I would email them details of each night's date and they would give suggestions about what to say and what not to say to keep this relationship on a healthy path. These guys would pray for us each week as well, and they were all pumped to meet Annia. I'd been in all of their weddings and they wanted (almost as badly as I did) for me to find someone. They were the ultimate dating coaches. It was a great bonding experience.

Anyway, I sat down and I typed these words:

🖂 I've never been one to kiss and tell, but because I have never kissed, I've never had anything to tell, but tonight I kissed Annia and...

Just as I typed the word "and' I got an incoming email from a guy named Chris.

Yup, that Chris. Her ex-boyfriend Chris.

From the beginning of the email, I knew things weren't right.

🖂 Hey man, I hate to be the one to break it to you, but I think we are being two timed here. I kissed her last night at the bar. Had sex with her the night before that. We didn't break up 9 months ago like she probably told you, we may not be "dating" but we are certainly "hooking up." The dating maybe gone, but the sex isn't. She is such a head case. One second she wants to be with me, the next she won't return my calls, but then we still find time to have sex. This is hard because I love her and want a relationship, but not anymore, knowing how involved she is with you.

I immediately rushed to the toilet and hovered there. An hour ago I was kissing the woman of my dreams... now, I found out she was having sex with Chris... a lot of sex, in fact! If she got drunk at the bar and had sex with him the night before and it was just a one time ordeal fueled by alcohol, I might have been able to forgive her more easily. But, it was clear, this was an ongoing ordeal with him.

Chris sent me texts, emails and such from her to him, all saying how she loved him, etc. That is when I knew it was all true. They were all time dated and stamped, so there was no easy way of faking that.

A big part of me wanted to think Chris was hiding in the bushes and saw us kissing and made the whole thing up to stop us from continuing to date, like a bad plot to a "Saved By the Bell" episode or something.

For the next hour, Chris and I messaged back and forth. Imagine that awkward conversation. We had both been played and both had our hearts broken by the same person. Neither of us were mad at each other. How could we be? We were both fed the same lie. Instead, we had a good conversation that was fueled with mutual respect for each other's pain.

The real question became… what next?

I told Chris that since he had been seeing her longer, that he should get first crack at confronting her.

That night I didn't sleep a wink. I stared at the ceiling, looking intently at the plaster like a message was about to become decoded in it and everything would suddenly all makes sense. Like in those puzzle books, when you stare at an image long enough that another image appears in 3D.

All night, I cried out to God. Why me? Why this? Why now? Was this some sick joke? Because I didn't find it funny at all.

At some point in the middle of night, Chris must have said something to her because at 5 a.m. she texted me frantically:

> 🖂 What is this about you talking to Chris? And why are you talking to him! He is such a jerk and trouble! What is going on?"

I sent her a copy of the texts and emails that Chris sent me where she declared her love for him and I asked, "How much of this is true, Annia?" It was dead silence for the next 5 hours. For a girl that texted me every five minutes for the last three months, to go to dead silence for the next five hours… that was when I knew for sure this was all true.

Eventually mid-afternoon she sent me an email.

In it, she admitted to it all. But, she didn't really apologize for anything. She was more "relieved" that the truth was now out there and that she no longer had to live a lie. She sent a similar message to Chris as well. She told me that she didn't love Chris. That it was just sex. That while she had this physical chemistry with him, that she connected with me on all other levels and then finally last night she let go of whatever walls she had and kissed me because she was ready to give her all to me in our relationship.

Chris and I talked again and compared our notes to try to make sense of it all.

I wish this is where the story ends… but it doesn't.

Or I should say, I should have ended things with her at this point, but I didn't.

I told Chris that despite this large bump in the road, I thought Annia was the gal I was supposed to marry. He told me the same, but that she had cheated on him once before as well and that this was the final straw… again, I should have cut my losses, but I didn't.

I told Chris that God can fix anything and he would fix this as well, she and I would be a story of God's redemptive grace, and how we had to let things get rough before He repaired things for his glory. Chris appreciated my heart and enthusiasm and bowed out.

I never spoke to Chris again after that, but I still wish him well to this day.

Oct 16th was day one of a nightmare that continued on for months…

I went to her apartment that night and picked up some things I left there, she put it all in a plastic sack on her front porch and left it there while she was still at work. I then went down to the playhouse to sell my tickets for that night's performance. It was freezing outside and my $300 tickets, I eventually let go for $80.

I was already over $2,000 invested into my first kiss, how could this get any worse I thought?

The drive home, all I did was cry. I went over that night to Keith and Sarah's house and we all sat at the dinner table, most of the time in silence, because we didn't know what to say. We were all confused.

A few days past, and we started texting each other. I told her I wanted to work this out, that I want us to go to a counselor and I tried and tried, but nothing, she wouldn't reciprocate.

I'd leave her alone, sometimes for weeks and then some days out of the blue, she would send these really twisted text messages; one Sunday I got this:

> 🖂 Today I wore the dress that I wore on our first date, I never wore it again because I just remember feeling like it was special for some reason. So I immediately put it away for safe keeping, like a wedding dress or something. I just wanted you to know that, that you are someone special to me. I hope you are doing ok?

The worst part was that, I sat in church that same morning, before she ever sent that text, and I saw a woman also wearing a dress similar to what she wore on our first date; of course, all I could do was think about Annia and the times we had together… so getting messages like that, they would manipulate me, I would start to think that the stars are aligning and that God wanted us to be together again and then I would contact her and it would be another brick wall.

I remember the dress conversation ended with a cold and confusing response:

> 🖂 I feel God is leading me to be back with you, but I keep fighting it, because I don't want it.

I was hurt.

> ✉ Why not? Why wouldn't you want to be with me? I loved you.

She responded,

> ✉ I don't know, I just can't explain.

...and this cycle continued, always ending in rejection.

I would continue to get messages like this and have conversations similar to this and it went nowhere each time.

After six months of this, she appeared again on the dating site we met on. She had always said she needed to work on herself over and over, and that dating was the last thing from her mind. I was so pissed about this I messaged her and she said the most twisted response:

> ✉ I feel I'm ready to date now. I've been on dates here and there. But I still come home alone and my roommate always says "ok, what didn't this guy have that Ryan has?" That's how strong an influence you had on me, you set the template for what I am seeking now. Your character and example are exactly what I strive to now find in a man.

I immediately replied:

> 🖂 Why do you want just a template, when you can have the original. I want you back!

And she said, same as always:

> 🖂 I know, some days I do too. But it just isn't right yet.

That night I threw my phone across the room. I was hanging out with Keith. He is one of those "slow to speak, quick to listen" types and he said "I know you want to make this work, but I don't. I can't stand her, with all that I am because of what she is doing to you. This manipulation game she is running. It's time to let go." After Keith said that, somehow, I realized he was right. Maybe God was finally convicting me or setting me at ease at that moment to finally let go.

The next day I did something that was long overdue. I decided to see a therapist about her. I sought council with my pastors and friends this whole time, but it was time for a fresh set of ears.

Through the therapy process which was intense (6 days in a row, 4 hour sessions each day) I learned a ton about myself and the situation. I'm glad I did it and would tell anyone to do the same. It made me more aware of situations in my life, and from my past, that I have let affect my perception of people I have encountered ever since. Through the process, I eventually learned how to avoid future relationship issues and have healthy communication with the people in my life.

After therapy, in many ways, it helped me control conversations with Annia in a more healthy manner.

A few months past and we didn't have contact, then she came to town with her cycling team (another one of her random activities and adventures) and told me that she just wanted to say hi. She didn't want to meet up, just that she was in town thinking of me. I offered to do lunch the next day, but she refused.

I told her that I wanted her to consider seeing my therapist to properly address her past and all the hurt she endured, this of course upset her and she refused, even after I offered to pay the bill to the tune of a $1,000. Somehow, I still cared about her that much. Some might say to that she still had control over me.

After that, again, I didn't hear from her for months.

The next time when she messaged me, she was taking a bus out of Lincoln and was headed to the West coast on a missions trip and sent me a nice message saying that she was thinking of me and happy times with me. I couldn't tell if she was baiting me to meet up or keep talking, so I gave a polite yet vague response back and we didn't talk again for a while.

When she got back from her missions trip, I messaged her some links to some things and we conversed about previously, eventually she told me about Todd her new guy and she told me that she was taking God seriously and His will in her dating relationships and even apologized for some things she did to me.

At this point… I felt like I was talking to a whole other person. It was clear that she was growing in her relationship with God too, thanks to her ministry studies no doubt.

As time passed, we'd send friendly messages here and there. We never talked about dating again, just friendship things.

There is a saying: when you love someone, you have to love all of them, not just some of them… that was how I felt about Annia. Despite the mistakes she made, I always made myself available to help or listen in some way.

Then the final heartbreak…

I remember the moment vividly still today because it was before Halloween, our mutual favorite season, she was working at her Halloween business and I was watching horror films, *Stir of echoes* that night in fact. Annia and I talked about this and as the conversation progressed to her and what was going on in her life, she was being vague and shallow. Again, knowing her the way I did, that was code for "something is going on".

Then I hit the pause button on the DVD player when she said something I wasn't prepared for…

🖂 I'm pregnant.

I immediately responded:

> ✉ Congrats! You're going to a great mom. You are so creative that your child will never be bored.

But then my heart broke when she told me:

> ✉ I cant' be a mom now. I'm too busy! I have an abortion scheduled in 4 weeks.

She told me and one other person at the time, because she thought I would listen and not judge… she and I are both adopted and Christians, so logic says giving birth was what should happen. I'm staunch pro-life; she on the other hand, obviously not. Her reasons for aborting were based in vanity, she admitted it, she didn't want to have to explain being un-wed and pregnant each day while working at her church; she was about to graduate with a ministry degree and also felt this would hinder potential jobs.

I pled with her; I told her that all those people would admire her more for giving life despite this and then giving that life to someone else as well… and then came the other catch, she said if she was to have a child that she would insist on keeping it and that she would never give it up the way she had been.

Then for the next four weeks, I fell into "save that baby" mode. I talked to her every day. I begged her to choose life.

My best friend Keith and his wife Sarah, received their first child through private adoption, one that I had a hand in setting up, so I figure that I could do some wheeling and dealing and find another family for Annia's child… and I did. But she rejected the offer. I then offered to pay her rent for a year if she kept her child; she still said no. I found private donors who were willing to pay all her medical expenses till she had the child and for a year after as well; she still said no. I met with pastors, friends, everyone- I pulled out all the stops to save that child.

For the four weeks leading up to the abortion, her and I talked about abortion and how it related to our mutual faith in Christ and she said that her faith, to which she was getting a degree in, was "pro choice" and gave biblical reasons why, I of course had an opposing view and we constantly clashed over this.

Todd, the father of the child wanted her to keep it. He wanted to be involved and was ready for fatherhood. He even went as far as to call all her friends the week before the abortion and tell them she was pregnant and about to abort. This enraged her. Several of her close friends disowned her over this too. She, however, pushed him out of her life immediately, just as things got tough in her life, much like she did with Chris and me. Instead of picking a guy and trying to repair things, she just tossed us aside and started over.

And she still went ahead with the abortion.

I tried to show her Christ's love in all this, so the day after the abortion, I sent her flowers with this verse attached:

"Give thanks to the Lord, for he is good. His love endures forever"

-Psalm 136:1

Her abortion crushed me.

I'm not sure why fully, but I think in large part because I felt my words had no impact on her anymore. If they did, then she wouldn't have gone through with it. Though I have been reminded that she was ultimately the one that made the decision and that I did all I could as a friend to be there for her, I still felt guilty. I felt I could have told her church where she worked and maybe they would have interfered; she might not have ever spoken to me again, but I might have saved that child. But then again, she still might have gone through with it regardless.

Annia and I talked here and there after that. In some ways, I think she realized that I was someone she really could trust. She also had a reduced friend count from this incident as well, so in the wake of her actions, I was among the few still standing by her side, despite that I was severally opposed to her choice.

It was nice having her in my life in a more active sense, or at least electronically.

I was taken aback when one day she asked me, "Are we ever going to be friends again? I mean real friends. The kind that hangs out." At the time, it was the winter holidays and I was lonely as always. Again, my friends are all married with kids, so I hardly see them at that time of year. So Annia invited me over for Christmas dinner. For some reason, I felt it wasn't my place to go. Then she invited me over for New Years Eve, and I said yes, not caring if it was dangerous for my heart or not.

I'm not sure why I went, other than so much time had passed and so many things had happened. I guess I just wanted to see her again face to face. I didn't know what I might feel. Our story had so many ups and downs that a big part of me wanted to see if I could be just friends with someone to whom I was still attracted.

So I went with her to this New Year's Eve party. It was everything I had hoped it would be. A typical night with Annia, filled with random adventures, including getting lost in a cornfield trying to find the house we were going to for the night, having to drive 45 minutes away, to the middle-of-nowhere-Iowa just to get to said house and having to baby-sit on top of this. These encounters with a sordid cast of characters that make up her life were just like any night with her. I loved the adventure of it all as always. But still it wasn't right in my own heart. Feelings were starting to return on my end that I knew I shouldn't entertain.

I got her back to her apartment by 2 a.m. and she asked if I wanted to stay on the couch.

A big part of me wanted to. I wanted to just keep talking to the one of the coolest people on the planet, I wanted to make breakfast together and sit on her porch like the old days and just talk while sipping tea… but I had this gut feeling that had I stayed… I would have eventually done something wrong.

So I said no, and I went home.

After that, she was really distant to me. I didn't know why, but I also didn't ask either. We didn't argue or disagree on anything that we talked about on New Years. I thought we were moving ahead with a better friendship. A couple of weeks later, she joined a dating site that I was on and we got into a fight.

I told her that I thought it was wrong that she was on there. She just had an abortion a month ago, she was graduating in three months and likely moving. So it seemed to me at least not the best grounds for starting a relationship. I thought she should have more time to herself to focus on future goals. Part of me said all this out of concern and anger for some other guy that would fall for her. She would have another frivolous relationship with and drop him at a moments notice, breaking his heart when she moved. Maybe it was a bit of jealousy too. Maybe it was frustration that she wasn't attracted to me anymore… who knows.

But when I told her my opinion (on her dating again) she got upset and told me off. She said that what she does and who she does it with was none of my business…

… and that is how things ended with Annia and me.

We never spoke again.

I learned a lot from my experience with her. When I said I felt the Holy Spirit come over me, telling me to "honor and protect her," I feel like I got a large lesson in that! I constantly tried to listen to her, to help her in whatever was troubling her daily. I loved her and I expected nothing in return, just her time and whatever came along with that, was a bonus.

I don't regret her being my first kiss; she was someone special and always will be, though I regret how much of my heart I carelessly gave away to her.

If there was a take away from her, it would be this. Some people just aren't ready to be honest with themselves. Ultimately, she wasn't. Through all the manipulations, misleadings, playing games with my heart and me foolishly allowing it, it only hurt us both. She had a lot of issues that she needed to address on her own before being in a healthy relationship. I did too, and had I not met her, I may have never went to therapy.

Maybe that is why God placed her in my life when he did. Annia taught me how to listen and respect someone that I was pursuing, but had I stayed with her, I would have just compromised myself as a person more and more, the further along we went.

After we broke up, every night for months as I laid down to pray I said "Jesus, wherever she is, keep her safe and let her be drawing closer to you."

I don't know where Annia is today.

From time to time, I pray that same prayer, and I wonder where she might be. I think of her on holidays like Mother's Day. I know that day must be hard for her heart, and although I don't know if she cares about me anymore or thinks about me anymore, I still care about her. And I still pray for her.

Chapter 2
Eight Men In An Igloo

My worst date of all time (so far) goes a little something like this…

My pattern of online dating seems to continue to lead me to trouble, but it's so convenient to use! So I tried a new site. I won't say their name, but let's just say, it claims to electronically harmonize people.

The site makes each member take a personality test that takes 45 minutes to an hour before you can ever get a look at any potential matches.

I first tried the site out a few years previous to this story and after I took the test, it said I wasn't compatible with any of its current members! So, I had taken an hour-long test for nothing.

So fast forward to this particular day, and you could say I was less than thrilled at the idea of taking that same test yet again, with the possibility of getting the same results!

But I was single and overweight at the time and had nothing else happening in life, so I went for it. I took the test, paid the money to subscribe and I was ready to meet someone.

One girl who caught my eye was Brooke. She was new to town, just graduated from college at a popular Christian university, so she had a lot of potential. She was cute and seemed to like sports, so I gave it the old college try and messaged her. No response, per my usual luck. So I wasn't shocked at all at this point.

The next day, I went to my buddy Kirk's house for a Husker football watching party... and low and behold, there she was! This is great, I thought. Now I don't have to worry about endless messages back-in-forth over a computer, now I can just talk to her face to face. I asked Kirk if he had an in or new anything about her and he didn't, he just knew that she was friends with a friend and Brooke was new to town as of two weeks ago... so I was going into this blind. Well, other than her profile's information that I remembered from the day before.

I approached her and said hi. I told her some things that I thought were cool about her and she asked how I knew so much about her and I told her from her dating profile of course. I told her that I messaged her yesterday and she started laughing and said that she isn't a paying member, so she hasn't read the message yet. So now I felt really stupid!

So I gave her the bullet points of my profile and then somehow, I was able to recover enough from my initial awkward introduction that she agreed to go out with me the next day. Apparently I won her over with my humor.

Overweight Ryan just scored a date with a cute girl. This was crazy!

She was a fitness freak and at the time obviously I was not, so she said she refused to eat carbs after 8 p.m. I didn't get off work till 6 p.m. So we agree to meet at 7 p.m. at Panera Bread. She would just have coffee (her idea) and I would eat overpriced sandwiches.

I dressed up and arrived at 7 p.m. and she was not there. I waited by the door for fifteen minutes and nothing. At this point, I though to myself that she seemed nice, so I wanted to give her the benefit of the doubt. She had my cell number, so should things have gone wrong, I assumed she would call. She could have gotten a flat tire or something, who knew? But again, I just kept telling myself, "Fat Ryan gets to spend time with a cute girl—let's keep thinking positive!"

So I went inside, ordered food and waited for her arrival. After I plowed through my meal, I ordered another meal to feed the beast and pass the time.

8 p.m. arrived and she was not there.

I should have left... but maybe I stayed to just prove to myself that someone who was actually that late, would in fact show.

8:45 p.m. she finally shows up.

A full hour and forty five minutes late! Now, remember, she said no carbs after 8 p.m., so even if she meant that she wasn't showing up till 8 p.m., she then was still 45 minutes late. With no call!

Regardless, she didn't even say sorry for being late.

She was kind of quiet and subdued, pretty much the opposite of the person I met the day before. She was actually really standoffish. We all have off days, I thought, so I let it slide and just kept at it.

Over the next hour, I would ask her questions that begged for an essay response and somehow she was able to magically turn them into yes/no answers instead. It was frustrating beyond comprehension.

If she wanted to go, she could have, but then again, so could I. So we both stuck around and 90 minutes in I asked what apparently must have been the worst question possible at this point:

"So, what is your favorite movie?"

Brooke fired back, "Oh that's right, someone mentioned that you are big into movies. I hate movies! I've seen maybe eight in my whole life. They are boring and a waste of time and money. Plus they are so loud in the theatres that I don't want to damage what hearing I have left. I assume you are asking this in hopes that I will rhetorically ask you the same thing?"

OUCH!

I lost it. I fired back "If answering this question is too daunting of a task than by all means, don't answer it!" I forged ahead. "I assume you are a book reader then, so maybe you'd like to share what your favorite books might be?"

She then belittled me by explaining that you can't have a favorite book because there are so many different categories of them, and that movies were far inferior because most movies are based on books and that the books included all the details that the film would miss.

I'm not sure why I asked this final question. I just blurted it out. I was just trying to shift gears and get out of movie talk before I lost my cool or got any more offended at her ignorance to the cinema… so I asked, "What was your favorite vacation?"

Her eyes lit up like a Christmas tree, her enthusiasm level grew exponentially, and she quickly responded with nervous excitement that now she got to share. "Oh, that's easy! That would be when I went on an Alaskan Wilderness Survival Adventure for two weeks."

I had a vision of what this might look like: killing a bear with her bare hands and eating it, fending off wolves for the scraps, using the bear's hide for a cover at night, and then cutting down trees and making a fire and foraging for berries, all while traveling the Alaskan landscape via dogsled.

I was also waiting for her to tell me that this where she found herself or something and had some great moment of realization, like the film (or book to her) *Into the Wild*.

She then explained the "best time of her life."

The Alaskan wilderness adventure involved her and eight guys building an igloo in the middle of nowhere and then for two weeks, staying inside it, sleeping in shifts and trying to stay warm by eating 8,000 calories a day through M.R.E.'s and all they had was a shovel and a portable, gas-burning stove for cooking and emergency heat.

I don't mean to come off as a pervert… but one girl and eight guys alone in the middle of nowhere… that sounds about as sketchy as it gets!

So, trying to keep a straight face was difficult to say the least. I asked, "What did you do in the meantime? I mean when you weren't eating or trying to stay warm in a sleeping bag. Did you go kayaking? Maybe hiking or something?"

She then explained they didn't leave the igloo for two weeks; the only time they did was to go outside to dig a hole to go to the bathroom in. That's what the shovel was for.

I was still not buying this or even understanding it. Why was this fun again?

Comedian Lewis Black often remarks that he thinks ice fishing is the dumbest thing a human being could do… I would like to contest that with this "Alaskan Wilderness Survival Adventure." With fishing, at least there is a goal, to catch a fish. With this survival adventure, since there are no sights to see, they all could have stayed home and turned the heat off on a cold day and gotten the same affect!

I then asked if she was close to the "Igloo Eight" today, since after all, they only had each other for two weeks. Did they at least play cards together or something to pass the time? She told me she doesn't talk to them anymore and no, they didn't even play cards together. They just sat with their own thoughts for two weeks with eight strangers…

Again, this sounds about as suspicious as it gets!

After this "vacation" story, the place was closing down and it was a good cue to exit.

I left thinking, what just happened? Met her at a football party, she was alive and happy. Remove her from a group of people and she was miserable?

After the date, I went to go play cards with some friends. Among them, my pal Craig. At the time, Craig and I were in the same boat, loved the Lord, same age, good job and still lived with his parents. Craig also didn't get many dates either, so he was bummed that mine turned out to be a wash and encouraged me to keep trying. The right one would come!

I'm happy to say, the story doesn't end here...

The next morning, I got an email from Brooke.

In it, she apologized for her behavior from last night and told me that she is not ready to date yet and that I was very polite and kind to her, and what happened last night was not my fault. She also opened up about her bitterness toward men because she got ditched at the alter... not once, but twice!

WOW! That had to be hard on someone's heart. I felt a little bit of sympathy toward her.

Three weeks later, Craig called.

"I met this awesome girl at church; it was her first time there. She is really cute, new to town and just graduated from this popular Christian university. We're going out this week!"

I was suspicious.

"Craig... does she have a birthmark on her right ear? Long red hair? Brown rim glasses?" I inquired.

"Yeah, that's her! Oh yeah, her name is Brooke!" Craig said enthusiastically.

"Dude, that's the same Brooke I went out with a couple weeks ago! Bail Craig! BAIL!" I pleaded.

But Craig didn't listen to me... and good thing he didn't.

They are now married. Have been for several years and have a child together. Craig is an upstanding guy, one of the few left and just the right person to care for her heart. I'm happy for them, truly.

I wonder though, if Craig finally got the real story out of her regarding that "Alaskan Wilderness Survival Adventure"?

Chapter 3
Build Me Up, Break Me Down

Nine months after things ended with Annia and after I completed therapy, a mysterious thing happened; suddenly women found me attractive!

Maybe it was because I finally had self confidence for the first time ever. Regardless, I went on a few "singular dates", which means you go out once, but there just isn't anything there; a few of those encounters were absolute disasters as well, but my future was looking up I thought. I went from getting one date in 34 years, to 8 in a year. That is progress.

Then, I went out with Jamie Green and little did I know a storm was coming!

Jamie was without a doubt the most beautiful woman I ever met as far as physical attraction goes. She had that timeless beauty look. Regardless of how and why we ended, which was ironic (you'll found out why I say that later), I will never take that distinction away from her.

I met her on a Christian-based dating website. I emailed her once, before I met Annia and she never responded, which again, I was not shocked by. I never thought that someone that attractive would give me the time of day. But now, I was a new man, with new self confidence. So I thought, yeah, I do in fact deserve a chance with someone of that high caliber of attractiveness.

Based on her profile, we were searching for the same things and if she really didn't care about looks, like most overtly attractive women do, then I figured I might actually have a shot.

In her profile, she talked about being a virgin and was super blunt about her expectations of a man as far as not expecting sex and wanting a man that wanted her mind first… well since I was in the "no-sex-till-marriage camp" too, then I figured that I might once again, have a shot.

So I wrote her a few paragraphs, telling her all the things I valued about her; I meant every word too!

She wrote back the next day and agreed to talk online, which we did. She interviewed me for an hour via instant chat and then agreed to let me take her out the next weekend.

Originally, she asked if I wanted to go church with her and her family that weekend (which in hindsight, was a warning sign of trouble ahead, but we'll get there in due time…)

The next weekend, July 13th was the day I took her to my favorite sushi joint and oh man, you have no idea!

She took my breathe away. She was immaculate! She wore this peach-colored dress and beaded flower designed headband and all kinds of interesting jewelry and she just was all kinds of interesting. It was clear she cared about her looks. I just wore a tie, so I felt under-dressed at best!

We talked for three hours.

She blew me away. She was intelligent. She loved Jesus. She loved serving people. We were almost the same age even. She was apparently impressed with my volunteer work too and my mind, so she saw all my good qualities.

We ended the date with getting ice cream, and we just sat and talked. I knew she was a cut above the rest.

I asked her, why she agreed to go out with me and she said smiling "You should have read your initial email you sent, your words were so passionate and genuine, that I knew you were different from the rest."

Laughing I quickly responded "Read 'em? I know what I said and I still mean every word too! You're awesome!"

She started laughing. As we walked by a fountain she pointed and I looked down and she asked if I saw some change in there and then as I leaned in, she splashed me! I was covered in water and that's when I knew I had her.

I walked her to her car and opened it's door and asked her out again and she said yes and I couldn't believe what just transpired! I got a woman who was a perfect 10 by all standards, both physically and as a person to go out with me and now for a second time coming up! My confidence was now at an epic level because I believed in myself. I knew I was a good guy and this woman saw it. She could have gone out with anyone, but she chose me!

My friends were ecstatic when I gave them the play by play of the date. "She actually likes you!" Melissa said.

Melissa is my "secret weapon" or my "dating coach" as I like to call her. She and her husband Paul are my dear friends. She is a psychologist, and to show you how big her character is, after Annia cheated on me, Melissa was the first to contact Annia, a person who she had never met and pleaded with her to meet, just to talk about this situation because she knew that for what had transpired, that there has to be something more going on behind the scenes.

After that, Melissa has always been willing to give advice and wants to know about my dating life so I don't run into another Annia. But with Jamie… even Melissa was blindsided!

It all started on date #2.

We decided that I would join her at her brother's basketball tournament and then we would go for a walk. Her brother had just turned 21 and was the youngest of the family; she also had 3 sisters—one older and two younger… and this is where it started to get weird, so please try to keep up.

All her sister's names start with the letter "J." Jessica, Jennifer and Jackie. All the men in the family—the father, his son, and even his son-in-law (Jackie's husband)—are all named James, Jamie's mother, Barbara, is the only first name in the family that doesn't have a "J."

So I arrived at the basketball court and it was game on (bad pun intended)!

The instant I arrived, young James walks up to me, no hand shake, nothing, just these words: "Hey man, can you run the score board?" Was I wearing a referee shirt? Did my Dickies shorts and buttoned up green/gray/yellow plaid shirt say "scorekeeper"? Well, I didn't want to be a jerk, but I was really looking forward to just sitting in the stands next to Jamie and bonding. James's girlfriend Kelsey (thank God, not another "J" name) urged me to do it, in front of Jamie, so I didn't want to look like a prick… so I agreed.

The referees sat me down and gave me a crash course in hand signals and some how I was running the scoreboard. Meanwhile, Jamie was sitting with Kelsey and cheering on James Jr.

The game ended and Jamie walked up to me and told me that I did a bad job since her brother's team lost. I said he should learn to pass more! She laughed and we headed over to another section of the bleachers where I met Jessica, her youngest sister; she was super friendly and fun and the typical youngest sister from a big family.

I also met her mother Barbara, who didn't pay much mind to my existence until Jamie eventually said we met on a dating site… after that, she looked at me with a cautious mother's eyes toward a potential suitor of her daughter's heart.

We all went to lunch and Barbara couldn't wait to interrogate me. I answered most of the questions correctly… I guess.

But the fun really began when she started talking conspiracies theories. Now, I believe in some of the standard ones… JFK, 9/11, aliens. But Barbara believes in all of them!

Further more, anything that goes wrong in the world, she blames the "Illuminati", which is supposedly this secret organization that does everything for Satan's better benefit and secretly controls everything, from our government, the media, whatever you will… now, I'm not sure how much of that I believe, but I was knowledgeable enough in the lore of it that at least that I could hold a conversation and Barbara became a fan of me at that point. Lunch was an hour and she talked easily 45 minutes of that on the Illumanti!

She also mentioned the HIV cure is readily available via some herbal pill from a popular multi-level marketing company. I had to bite my tongue hard from laughing at that one.

Oh, and it doesn't stop there… she later went on to tell me that the secret savior of the world is Russian President Vladimir Putin and to top all this, that she and various members of the Green family are in a "secret prayer group" that organize and gather on Sunday nights and pray specifically to stop the Illumanti and that a prophet named Anita Johnson receives visions from God on the Illumanti's weekly evil deeds and plans.

This was a bit much to process.

And this was just date #2!

Missing from this gathering was the patriarch of the family, James Sr. who was a farmer and pastor. I asked where he was, and they said he was working on their new house and praying. I inquired more on this, and Barbara and the daughters explained that they were building a house to shelter runaways as well as their whole family. The kicker was that they were constructing it from scratch and not hiring out any of the work. So James Sr. would pray for days about what he should do next, and when he felt that God had revealed to him how or what to do (dry-walling, for instance), then he would have at it. The smart aleck in me challenged this logic by recommending the obvious—Googling it or looking it up on YouTube But they responded that by doing that, they weren't living by faith... I appreciated their heart and spirit on this... but I thought that was a bit much!

I shared that I spent time constructing homes in New Orleans after Hurricane Katrina, and I could see by the looks on their faces that suddenly my stock had risen.

At lunch, they also remarked at their dissatisfaction that I didn't pray in tongues; they even went as far as to tell me later that I need to pray in tongues so Satan couldn't hear my prayer requests and use my wants against me... I'm not knocking on the religious practice of "speaking in tongues", but it just isn't something I've felt led to ever participate in. But this would be a sore spot with the Greens for weeks to come.

After lunch, we went back to the gymnasium to watch James Jr. attempt to do some more balling. On the way there, Jessica said "Are you going to run the scoreboard again?" I thought she was joking, but then Barbara and Jamie chimed in that they appreciated my "servant's heart" so after that, I kind of had to do it. But all I really wanted was to actually talk to Jamie without others around.

Game Two started and once again, I sat alone, watching her brother the ball hog attempt to guide his crew of misfit players into oblivion. As this debacle on the court unfolded, I noticed two people walk into the gym who certainly carried a presence: it was Jennifer and James Sr., the two branches of the Green family tree I had heard so much about.

Jennifer was a former model and dresses up for any occasion. And she gets noticed. A rivalry between her and Jamie was apparent as well. They were always trying to one up each other to the point that they secretly felt contempt for one another. Jennifer was also extremely blunt. She is the kind of person who will walk up to a stranger and critique them with comments that are border-line rude, whether she realizes it or not! I would know. I was the recipient of several of those comments at numerous awkward times.

Her father was quiet and stern. On any given encounter, he never said more than five words to me. On any given day, I couldn't tell if he was ready to give me a handshake or a bullet to the head.

As the game wound down, Jamie came to check in on me and said, "Would you like to meet my dad?" Sure, I thought. I had already met Barbara, so why not? I've practically met the whole family on date two anyway.

I walked up to James Sr. and our first interaction was awkward to say the least:

"Please to meet you, Mr. Green" I started.

"Who are you, and what do you do here?" he replied.

"Well, I'm Ryan and I ran the scoreboard here today." I felt awkward.

This was not going how I had wanted to introduce myself.

"Well, you didn't do a good job, because my son's team lost," he remarked sternly. I couldn't tell if he was joking or not.

"Well, your son should have passed the ball more!" I said, trying to diffuse the already awkward conversation with humor.

Except, unlike Jamie… he didn't laugh at my joke!

He then turned his head to Barbara, like a king no longer amused by the court jester; now he was debating if I was to get my head cut off, or taste his food first for poison, or if I was allowed to walk away and live to joke another day.

My semi-saving grace came when Jennifer (remember, I have never met her before) walked up with Jessica and said, "So, I hear you're good at roofing. Well, Father needs help with that." She looked at her sister. "You should come by on Saturday and lend Father a hand. We can't pay you in money, but we'll pay you in good food and attractive women." She grinned.

That's right. No "Hi, I'm Jennifer," no "What's your name?" She just went straight into her agenda. Also, they called Mr. Green "Father" a lot. Of course, that is his title, that is what he is. But on the side of the tracks I grew up on, I called my father "Dad" and when we called him Father, it was always in a formal context where he wasn't in it. When the Green family members said "father" though, it just rolled off the tongue strange to me. It made me feel like they were part of some exclusive little club: "Father, can I borrow that chair?" "Thank you, Father, for the ice cream."

The real hilarity came when after Jennifer proposed this roofing idea, Jessica and her flirty self started in and Barbara joined the pow wow, and James Jr. and Kelsey were in earshot, and I was kind of starting to feel suffocated, so I blurted out, "Look people, this is just the second date! Jamie might want to cut me after this, so let's not get too excited here!" Everyone laughed.

"You have a sense of humor, too?" remarked Jennifer. "Oh, you're a keeper!"

After that, I walked Jamie to her car, followed by her whole family.

It was still awkward. Was I dating Jamie? Or the Green family?

After that, nearly every date we had in the next three months included one or more of her family members. There is a saying, "you don't just marry the girl, you marry the family." In this case… that was pretty spot on.

The "Green girls" as I called them would text me often, not just Jamie. So, I felt like I was becoming part of their exclusive club.

Jamie, though had a leg up from other candidates for my heart. For one, she actually met some of my friends and so it made things a bit more real, unlike Annia.

Jamie worked insane hours. An eight hour day was a slow day for her; several days a week, she would pull ten, twelve, even fourteen hour days. She and her sisters ran a boutique. They did well for themselves. Jamie was the queen bee of the operation.

I'd text her every other day. I'd send her cute and fun pictures just try to brighten her day. I also stepped up my game: flowers every week for her. If not, then some kind of food that she could share with the sisters. Once when I couldn't see her that upcoming weekend, I bought manicures and pedicures so that she and her sisters could go out and make a day of it on me. I was going to win this woman's heart if it was the last thing I did.

One week I was late in my flower delivery, so at 1:30 a.m., I got up and drove an hour to get to her house and leave the flowers on her doorstep before she woke at 4 a.m. to get to the gym. I had a jungle's worth of flowers waiting for her. I scored big points that day!

I also spent two times more money on her than I did on Annia, but at the time I didn't care, because I felt this was the one that God wanted me to slave over. She demanded perfection and I was for sure going to give her my best attempt at it.

However, there were a few cracks in the foundation. As much as I did things for her, she didn't do much of anything for me. No surprise lunches, or random phone calls or even just a card that let me know that I was doing a good job. At least Annia gave me a card.

She did pay for tacos and chips once, one night's dinner, a whole $12!

My friends started to notice this too. Melissa was the most concerned. She'd look at Jamie's texts to me and tell me, "She is showing interest in you, time and time again. But there is some kind of wall that is still in the way".

The end came after a great day at the lake. The Greens invited me to go jet skiing, and we all had laughs and good conversations. I really felt like I was part of something special, or at least I was made to feel that way. Mr. Green, after three months still said five words or less to me, but he at least started shaking my hand. That was progress, I thought. But Jamie was starting to pull away. I could feel it.

The day at the lake was a victory of sorts for me. The thing is, though I've lost a lot of weight, I'm still not comfortable with my body. I also have some over grown cartilage on my chest that I got teased for massively as a kid, so because of that, I never take my shirt off in public. Not even when I swim.

It had been ten years, if not longer since I even went swimming; the only time I actually do, is when I know my very close friends are around to have my back. The cartilage is a massive insecurity, but I knew this would come up with Jamie at some point, so I hit the issue head on and went to the lake knowing they would notice. I figured if they were going to let that affect them, then they were idiots. They knew I was a good guy, so if they were going be put off by my physical appearance, then they needed to get a life.

I survived the day at the lake. Whatever insecurities I had going into that day were all for naught. No one mentioned the cartilage on my chest. We all seemed to get along well, laughing and talking. We spent a lot of time on the water—tubing, jet skiing, and just hanging out on the boat. I got hurt after getting tossed from a jet ski (I would later learn I had broken a rib, and it took over eight weeks to heal), but other than that, it was a good day. Despite their awkwardness, I was starting to feel a kinship with them. Jamie's distance, although still there, seemed like maybe it was just part of her personality. I walked away from that day thinking, if this is a snap shot of my life, then it's looking pretty good. I just needed to get Jamie to open up to me.

When Jamie was away from her family, she was almost entirely a different person. She'd open up about a lot of pain and stress she had in her life and about these almost unattainable expectations she felt others put on her, and that she put on herself as well. There wasn't a day when we were alone together, she wouldn't break down and cry over the stress she felt from her family.

I tried my best to help, but most of my suggestions fell on deaf ears.

Then one day, she texted me and told me she was pulling the plug. She didn't want to see me anymore.

However, she agreed to meet and talk a few days later and try to be friends… So we spent a Saturday together and just hung out… But with Jamie, there was another catch… Much like Annia (except for our last day together), we weren't physically involved at all. We agreed from the start to try to keep that part at bay for as long as possible. I would have waited till our wedding day to kiss her had she asked. I respected her that much… but after three months of dating, I was looking forward to at least some hand-holding action or something. I wanted some sort of sign that she felt something for me.

That last day together, we went for a walk and flew a kite, and I took her to my friend's restaurant (which isn't cheap) and I treated it like any other day. Honestly, she opened up even more than she ever did before. It was like once I got banished to the "friend zone," she liked me more, maybe because there wasn't an expectation of having to provide something affectionate.

She told me things that made me hurt for her. Like about how emotionally distant of a relationship she really had with her parents and how she was constantly having to compete with her sisters. She broke my heart though when we spent the night just talking in my car. I was going to drop her off, but we sat in her driveway for nearly two hours talking. At one point, I felt frustrated and confused. "If you can talk to me about all this stuff, why aren't we dating? Why don't you want to be with me?"

She looked at me sadly. "Here is the thing." She took a deep breath. "You are a 'Hallmark guy', like the kind of guy we women see and root for in those Hallmark movies. You are perfect in so many ways." I could tell she was being genuine. "You love God, love others and have such a big heart. I can tell you anything and you are so smart. You come up with the greatest ideas!" I was still confused. If I was so great, then why was she breaking up with me? She continued, "Father warned me that men would want me for my money and my possessions, and you are the first guy I've met that I know could care less about what I have."

I couldn't resist asking the obvious question. "Then why don't you want me in your life, Jamie? All I want is you! Your family is a bit eccentric—" she laughed at this. "But this is what I want—you and me, just talking like this, every day

Then she said the one thing that was like a dagger to my heart. She looked me straight in the eyes and said, "Honestly, it's because of one thing. I'm not physically attracted to you."

My pierced heart sank deeper into my chest. After those words, I knew there was nothing more I could say. I had no more case to plead. It was a battle I had just lost the will to fight. We talked a little bit longer, but it wasn't long before I was alone in the car, driving back home.

All I could hear, over and over in my head, was, "You're ugly" My biggest fear just came alive again. I've been ugly or overweight all my life. I didn't get a real date till I was 34 and now I felt like I just went from taking two steps forward, to a hundred steps back.

I wish this is where I could tell you the story ends, but I'm a glutton for punishment, apparently, and much like with Annia, I once again tried fixing the unfixable.

Here is the thing: by some people's standards, the Green's were crazy. But as I told my friends, they were my kind of crazy. I think they have good hearts; it's just that sometimes they execute that wrong, that's all.

As I said, there were two versions of Jamie: the one with her family members around and the one without. Underneath all the makeup and exterior polish, she was a real person and that is who I fell for.

So, the salvage effort began.

A month after we ended, I wrote her a nine page love letter. That took five hours to do by the way. Two hours to write, an hour to spell-check and proof read and then two hours to transpose to paper. I even went out and bought five different types of pens: I wanted the ink to look and be absolutely perfect. It was the most daring thing I have ever done to that point for a woman. I originally caught her attention with my words, so I went at it once again, hoping she would read the sincerity and passion in them.

Two weeks later, I had heard nothing back.

Originally, I wasn't upset; I figured she was taking all that I said to heart and was processing it all. Maybe she was really praying about all that I said in that letter, just like I asked her to do.

Another week past and her mom randomly emailed me. Now, this was odd because her mom and I hadn't spoken on a regular basis other then our paths crossing when I was with Jamie. I spoke to the other Green sisters regularly when I was with Jamie, but never her mom.

Her mom invited me to the family's church and then out to lunch with them after. She said that the upcoming week's message would be something I would like.

I was taken aback, because the Green's often did things without letting Jamie know. So I was curious as to what Jamie thought of this? Did she even know? Better yet… did the Greens know about the nine page love letter?

I texted Jessica for the first time in a month and asked:

> ✉ Does your mom know Jamie and I have broken up, and if so, why did I get asked to come to this gathering?

Jessica always told me the truth, so I had no reason to worry when she replied:

> ✉ It's no big deal, you should come, we all miss you! I'll even save you a seat ;)

I called Melissa and we conferred. We both were dumbfounded. This was so unorthodox. Why would they invite an ex-boyfriend to a family event? Melissa thought it was wise to break the silence and contact Jamie and tell her what her mom was up to. So I did and she said that she would like me to come and that it would be nice to catch up… so I took that as a sign that I should go. Fact was, I would have regretted it otherwise and wondered "what if" for the rest of my life.

So that weekend I went.

I arrived at the church five minutes early and there was no one there yet. It was just myself and Mr. Green. Who walked up right to me and engaged me in a conversation about the weather, farming, racial relations, football and the Illuminati. He spoke way more than five words. I was shocked. He acted like the prodigal son had just returned! He asked me where I had been, and I didn't know what to say. Should I tell him Jamie dumped me, so I was onto other things? It was just a weird question in the first place!

At that exact moment, Jessica walked in and ran up and hugged me just before I had to answer him. I was relieved to not have to answer Mr. Green's twenty questions. The church seated 75, but maybe twelve people were there, including the Green family.

I sat next to Jessica, while Jennifer and Jackie sat two rows ahead. But Jamie was nowhere to be found.

Church started and no band or hymn books were around; instead the worship music was played off a CD. I quickly realized the majority of the words were in Hebrew, and stopped trying so hard to sing along. Twenty minutes into the music, I felt a hand rub my shoulder with a "Hi, it's good to see you. You look great." It was Jamie. She sat right next to me for the whole service. Jessica sat a chair apart, and all other eleven people were sort of scattered. Again, there were 75 open seats, but Jamie sat right next to me.

After church, the Greens gravitated toward me, the outsider, as well as the four people in the room I didn't know… it started to feel very *Children of the Corn* like! Either way, an older couple, Dean and his wife Jean, walked up and introduced themselves. Jamie stepped in and told them, "This is Ryan, one of my absolute closest friends." Dean and Jean immediately began to interrogate me. Not in a friendly chit chat way, but in an awkward, intrusive way. More on that later.

At this point, lunch couldn't come soon enough.

I went to lunch with the Greens; Dean and Jean followed and we had a picnic in the park. It was also my first chance to really talk alone and face to face with Jamie, though briefly. It was good to see her. It was like it always was with us. I missed her. She made no mention of the nine page love letter though, so I didn't know what she was thinking about me or maybe the possibility again of us.

Lunch was nice overall. We talked the usual subjects—the decline of Western civilization, Whitney Houston being murdered by the Illumanti, various "false flag attacks," and of course, Vladimir Putin.

Jennifer, always the one to start an awkward conversation, said toward the end of the lunch, "So someone left flowers on my car this morning and didn't leave a note." She glanced slyly at me. "Who would do such a thing?

Jokingly I responded "Oh, that's because I forgot the card at home. Sorry about that!"

Jennifer shot back, "NO. You don't get credit for these flowers. I remember the flowers you would get Jamie." I began to feel uncomfortable again. "You have taste. These were cheap and poorly thought out. They don't get the distinction of being a 'Ryan bouquet'. I could only be so lucky to receive one of those!" Everyone broke out in a nervous laughter.

Jamie left the lunch shortly after that to get ready for some family photos (which, apparently, they do on a monthly basis). As she left she said her goodbyes and then said to me "Bye, Ryan, it was good to see you… don't be such a stranger." This girl had me so confused.

Then a week later, things took an even more awkward turn…

Jennifer called and asked me to join her and help work on the new house they were building, or the "Green Family Compound" as I jokingly started calling it. It looked like something David Koresh would have envied.

I spend the day with Jennifer and her parents working on various things on the house. Jamie was nowhere to be found. Nor did we talk about her. We just talked about life and did construction… then at the end of the day, Barbara and Jennifer sat me down and Barbara spoke first.

"Ryan, I want you to know that we brought you here under alternative motives"…

"Uh, ok?" I nervously replied.

Barbara continued, "I know that you love Jamie. I can see it your eyes and in the way you treat her. The fact is, we want you to marry into this family. We think you are great. We are working on Jamie, trying to get her to have a change of heart." And then it got weird. Barbara matter of factly said, "Jamie is "Plan A" but should she not come around we have a "Plan B" lined up."

At this point, I thought she was about to offer up Jennifer or Jessica as potential brides. Knowing these people so far, this would have not shocked me!"

Do you remember Dean and Jean from church last weekend?" Barbara asked.

Fearfully, I responded with a "yes," half expecting Barbara to then offer up Jean and then a subsequent invitation into polygamy, because again, nothing would have shocked me at this point!

"Well, Dean and Jean have a daughter Katherine, who we think would be a good fit for you too" Barbara said.

"And if that isn't enough, I have Plan C, my friend Suzanne," Jennifer added.

All of a sudden, I'm a contestant on "The Bachelor" or something with the Green Family Compound as the backdrop. I half expected a limo filled with girls and Chris Harrison to appear from around a corner!

Now, let's take stock in this… the family of the woman I was in love with just told me they approve of me and want me to marry into the family. That's pretty wild! This was the first time I had met a girlfriend's family, and I had made such a good impression that they want me to sign on for the rest of my life. I was fairly flattered at this point.

Then it crazier…

Jennifer spoke up again. "Now, to execute these plans, we need to do something about your clothes because your sense of style is terrible, and if you are going to catch Jamie's eye again, we need to change everything about you." I realized she just meant my clothes, but still.

We literally got in the car after that and drove to the mall.

Again, I wish this is the part of the story where it ends. Where I put my foot down and say "enough is enough," but I was a fool in love and went along with Jennifer's plan.

We went to The Buckle and before walking in, Jennifer made me give her my credit card and promise to not complain and not look at a single price tag.

Now, let me state this. Up until then, I thought I dressed okay. I dress to be comfortable. None of my friend's wives complained about my clothes when discussing what might be holding me back from finding someone, so I thought I was doing okay in this area of life. I never paid more than $30 for Levi jeans or $40 for a button down shirt.

So after 45 minutes, I walked out of The Buckle with two shirts, a sweater and a pair of jeans for $400! The jeans alone were $160. Oh man, I almost threw up when I got home. But I'll concede, I did look good! It was tough; I looked nicer, but that money could have been spent in wiser ways. However, I put my trust in Jennifer, because after all, she was a personal stylist and ex-model, so she knew her stuff.

That night I went and treated Jennifer to dinner, and I asked her why she was doing this for me, because I knew she hated Jamie with a passion. Jennifer went on to tell me about the rift they had. I of course heard Jamie's side for months and it was sad seeing two sisters who were once so close let mutual pride stand in the way of them re-connecting. Jennifer said, "I may hate my sister, but I still want the best for her… and Ryan, your it. We all love you. Now, go get her!"

At that point, I wasn't sure if I was trying to win Jamie's heart for me or to not let the Green family down.

Barbara set up a dinner party for two weeks later. This was going to be my big debut of the "New Ryan".

I couldn't make up this next part if I even tried.

So I wore the sweater and Rock Revival jeans that Jennifer picked out… I made it to the venue early. I looked good, felt good, and I was ready to impress Jamie. As the guests arrived, first was Jessica, who was wearing the exact same brand and style of jeans as me but in a slightly different shade. Then came the oldest sister Jackie and her husband James, both sporting, you guessed it, the same jeans.

However, her husband James and I had the same shade. Then came James Sr. and Jr. Yep, you guessed it, the exact same jeans! If you're tallying this up, that's seven people wearing the same brand of jeans. There could be little doubt. I was officially a member of the cult. Someone please pass the Kool-Aid with cyanide right now!

As the party continued, finally Jamie walked in. She was not wearing jeans. She was wearing a dress. She made her rounds and came up to me. I was sitting next to Jessica and having some laughs with her and her new boy toy/ flavor of the week, Donovan. Everyone at the party complimented the fact that I looked nice and put effort into things... so I was expecting from Jamie an equally outstandingly positive review of the "New Ryan."

She looked me over and said, "So, I see my sister dressed you."

OUCH!

Though true, she could have at least followed it up with "You still look nice, though." But she didn't. I was crushed.

Our hero will not be detoured easily, though.

Her mother set up another dinner party, and I was going to go shopping on my own this time. I would buy a new outfit and blow Jamie out of the water because of the fact that Jennifer had no hand it. Melissa came along as an observer. I picked the outfit and she approved. For a vest, shirt and tie—$200. But at this point I didn't care about my spending. I was trying to win back Jamie, the pinnacle of women. I had two weeks to prepare to impress again.

At this point, Jamie and I had started communicating again. I'd text her nice things, cute animal pictures, inspirational verses and quotes; sometimes she would ask for my business ideas and sometimes she would even open up about personal things and struggles.

The night of the dinner party arrived, and I was ready to debut "Ryan 2.0." As I walked in, she did at the same time. Perfect, I thought. She and I alone—time for me to seize the moment! To top it all off, she was wearing the exact same color scheme as me. We beyond matched and complimented each other; I thought this might be the moment it clicked for her that I actually looked good because we had the same tastes. So I joked, "I see we have the same personal stylist" She fired back, "No, my sister doesn't dress me."

I responded, "Actually Jamie, I picked this outfit myself. I got it at Express."

"Oh," she said. "Well, I hate that store." She looked annoyed. "Lets head inside." I was again crushed. I hadn't even made it in the door without being rejected again.

After that, I silently gave up. I didn't even text Jamie. I just stopped.

From time to time, I'd hang with her sisters here and there, or help the Greens on the compound. But I started to realize something. Seldom did they ask me to hang out unless they needed something or wanted something in return. I was starting to feel used.

Another blow came when I was out building the compound one day, and the Greens knew I was feeling defeated with the lack of progress in the situation with Jamie. They then started quizzing me about my relationship with my church, my work and people in general, and then casually informed me that part of my problem was that I have a "bastard curse" because I was adopted. They explained that I did nothing to deserve this (much like salvation); I just got it because I was adopted. I could hardly believe what I was hearing. They politely informed me that the next ten generations of my children would carry this as well. Of course, they generously offered to cast it out through a speaking-in-tongues-infused prayer session. I didn't even know what to say in response. The whole conversation was so ridiculous. I was offended, but the whole thing seemed so crazy I wrote it off the same way I did their obsession with the Illuminati, and Barbara's love of Vladimir Putin. I probably should have just cut them out of my life at that point, but remember—glutton for punishment here. I still went back every now and then to help if they asked.

Eventually, though, the Greens started to get on my case more and more about the fact that I didn't pray or speak in tongues. In fact, they acted like I was beneath them spiritually because of this. More and more, I felt like an outsider; the people I thought had been rooting for my success, now seemed to be trying to program me to be the perfect husband for Jamie, tweaking me a bit here or there to fit the mold of what they thought she needed, while she was off dating other guys and keeping me at bay.

Two months passed and randomly, Jamie called me.

She asked me to come to dinner with Jessica and Kelsey one day after work. Curious and still very single, I agreed. At this dinner, she picked my brain for business ideas and we talked for a few hours, and then she apologized for being a jerk to me and for keeping me at arm's length. I was kind of blown away. I felt like I was talking to a new person and the fact she apologized in front of people spoke to me.

I thought my prayers were being answered, that her call to me was an obvious sign from God that things were going to work out.

But it wasn't long after I helped her again with some business stuff, that I began to feel like I was wasting my time. She wasn't taking any of my suggestions, and I was starting to feel used again.

So I didn't contact her for another month.

Eventually Jennifer and Jessica, who I still was in contact with, let it slip that Jamie had been dating someone for some time. I wasn't shocked by this. Jamie and Jessica both tried on men like clothes. A new weekend, a new date and a new potential suitor. However, unlike Annia, they were not promiscuous; the instant the men looked like they were seeking just "that one thing," they were eliminated. But that's what didn't make sense to me. I wasn't seeking "that one thing" with her. So why was she turned off by the companion she could have had in me?

Either way, word then came that she was single again. I figured it was time to give it one last shot.

Jamie loves Disney and fairytales in general. So I made her a story book. That took a ton of effort (it is hard work to make every sentence rhyme). In this fairytale, I was a prince who rescued her from her time-consuming job, and I told of the adventures we'd had and of all of the attempts I had made so far to win her heart. Then I commissioned my artist friend to draw pictures for each page. This thing was epic.

But before I spent $200 on these custom drawings, Melissa stepped in.

"Ryan," she said gently, "we know how bad you want this to work and I have to be honest, this might be the most romantic thing you've done yet. But," she shook her head. "This girl doesn't deserve it. She appreciates nothing about you. You emotionally give to her. You feed her with texts and positive words. So of course she likes you! You're always there for her." She paused. "But something is holding her back from loving you. And it sucks because she seems solid otherwise."

I took a week to think about my next move.

The next week, another surprise. Jamie called me just to talk. We talked for an hour about some personal struggles she was having. She could have talked to anyone and she chose me! I was on a high again.

Melissa even got in on the action. She and Paul just bought a new house. Jamie's best friend outside of the family is Erika. The two of them generally hang out all day on Tuesdays, like clock work. So Melissa hired Erika's cleaning company, to clean the new home. So Jamie dropped by with Erika when she came to give them an estimate, and this was the first chance for Melissa to secretly meet the person we had been talking about for months. Jamie didn't suspect a thing. After this initial meeting, Melissa's first reaction was, "Now that I've met her, I see why you are in love with her. She really is a great person--intelligent, poised and kind."

Her encouragement gave me the confidence to make another move. I would simply send an email. It was three pages and I stated my case as to why she needed to let me into her heart. I even said those dreaded three words: "I love you." I really meant it. Short of cutting my ear off, I think I showed her enough proof that I wouldn't forsake her.

And somehow, the email worked!

After seven months of trying, she finally agreed to go out with me.

Two weeks later, we went out. That of course wasn't without a catch. She called me a few days before our date and informed me that her mom wanted to tag along. Seriously. I told her an emphatic no. If Barbara had to come as a chaperone, than I was out. This night was for Ryan and Jamie alone!

I planned to take her to dinner and a movie. She loves fairytales, so I took her to *Cinderella.* I would have rather watched grass grow, but I'd endure for her. It was time to impress.

We went out, and it was bad.

From the instant she arrived, she was cold and stand-offish. It was as if she showed up out of pity and not because she genuinely wanted to be there.

She bailed on the dinner idea, and we settled for a drink before the show. I was not thrilled at all. So we "talked" for 45 minutes and then went to the movie. All I wanted to do was talk to Jamie, and now that time was being cut short. From a nice sit down dinner to vague chit chat before a movie, to seeing a film (which is not the most talkative of events).

At the bar, frustration set in. I asked if she knew all the efforts that I've done just to be with her and she said she didn't. Turns out, her family wasn't really "promoting" me all that much like they said they were. She also had no idea of Jennifer and me shopping for her specifically. She knew Jennifer and I went shopping, but not that it was to try to win her over with the style change.

At this point, she got angry. And the fact that her mom approved of me so highly only made it worse. I found out that anger came in part because of an ex-boyfriend she dated for several years. Her mother selected him for her, and Jamie stayed with him out of fear of her mom's disapproval. I reminded Jamie that we had found each other first on the dating site, and the fact her family was on board (sort of) was just a bonus. At least, for me.

I realized, as we were talking, that I didn't see any joy in her eyes. Not any happiness. She looked like she was serving time in prison by being with me. I walked her to her car and then we said our goodbyes. I knew in my heart of hearts that this really was goodbye.

The next day I sent her a text. I thanked her for giving me another chance. She wrote back saying she didn't know what the future held for us other than a friendship. I then wrote her a final email and said that if she really wanted me as a friend in her life, then she would have to call me and seek me out. I left that next morning for a missions trip for a week and told her that I'd really enjoy getting some dinner and telling her all about it when I got home… but I would wait for her to contact me and show me that she wanted me in her life.

To no one's shock, I never heard from her again.

In the end, all Jamie did was build me up and then break me down. It was as if she intended for me to feel special because I got to stand in her presence, but then was happy to toss me in the garbage and make me feel like such trash, time and time again and I was just supposed to take it.

Today I don't talk to the Greens either. I've ran into them by chance a few times at some local events. We shake hands and exchange vague pleasantries, but that's all. They aren't bad people; they are just eccentric at times and merely share different passions and convictions than I. While we share many things in common, they express their fervor for them differently.

I don't know where Jamie is today. But wherever she is, I hope she has an open heart for once and that whatever guy she is with now, she is allowing him to speak truth into her life and that she is growing with God regardless.

I learned a lot during my time with Jamie and her family, but if I had to narrow it down, it would be this: just be yourself. I was trying too hard to be something that I wasn't. I was trying too hard to be accepted, not just by her, but by her family as well. I shouldn't have to change the way I dress or the things I say to get people to like me for who I am. Period! Otherwise, any time a woman comes along and sticks around on a permanent basis, I'd be changing every aspect of who I am just to make her happy. I should be happy as well. You can only be a chameleon for so long. Change isn't easy; in relationships, we should be willing to change or adapt if there truly is something about us that makes us less desirable as a person, not just as a romantic partner. But I learned, what is inside is what counts. I had good insides, even Jamie saw it, so did her family, but sometimes people aren't ready to fully embrace who you are, they just can't get past the exterior and that's okay. Ultimately, be who you are, own it and eventually the right person just might come.

Jamie and I, as well as her family for that matter, we may speak in different tongues (pun intended), but we are both headed for the same eternal home. Maybe there, things will get sorted out and we'll learn to fully appreciate each other.

Chapter 4
Consider a Background Check!

Ever had a bad first date? Well, probably not like this!

I've had many misadventures with Shaun, one of my two best friends and someone I've known for twenty years now. We've done a lot of dumb stuff in our time. Once, we rode a golf cart at max speed and then went down a steep hill and he sharply turned, ejecting me from it. I hit my head, suffering a concussion. It looked like something the crew from "Jackass" would do. After blacking out, I woke to Shaun hovering over me, laughing and not alarmed at all. No "Hey man, you alive? You okay?" or something like that. Nope, just laughter.

Shaun may do some careless stuff and I'm usually the recipient of the consequences, but he has a heart of gold and has been by my side through the good times and bad, like few others. He is like a brother to me.

But, he still owes me an apology for this one.

One Tuesday night, Shaun was over hanging out, and we were about to indulge in our traditional "Crappy Movie Tuesday", which involved going to the video store and renting the three crappiest movies we could find and then trying to find humor in them. We've had some major laughs over the years doing this.

Before we were about to partake, he was using my AOL instant messenger (remember that?) to talk to Bailey, his then-girlfriend (now wife) and telling her goodnight so we wouldn't be disturbed on "guy night".

He was also talking to another friend. Still under my account mind you!

"Um, who is pinkkittypanama"? I asked.

"Oh that's Felicia." He said. "She's friends with Bailey. We're setting up this party for this weekend. I'd invite you, but I can't," he remarked.

"Whatever, dude. So what's the story with Felicia?" I inquired.

"Actually, I wanted to set you up with her," he responded. "I've actually been working on her in secret for you. She saw your band, so I think she is into the rock star thing. Only problem is, she has been seeing this guy Darren off and on for like five years." He hesitated. "So I hadn't really done anything because I don't want you to go out with someone who is still attached to someone else." I understood, and that was that.

A couple of weeks passed and Shaun mentioned that Darren was confirmed to be out of the picture, for some time now too apparently, so now it was time to act. So I instant-messaged Felicia, to get to know her and finagle a date for a few days later.

The thing that I find attractive the most in women, or at least the first thing I notice, is their hair. If a girl has some sexy hairstyle or coloring job, I instantly want to know more!

Felicia was about to go to cosmetology school. That sounded great to me. If things panned out, she'd likely always have more cool hair styles to model for me, so it would never be a dull day in that department.

We met up, got to talking and she was flirty and fun. From what I could tell early on, she had a dangerous side to her, but I found that intriguing, so we kept talking. Well, as I kept getting to know her, she essentially admitted she was still with Darren, but was looking to trade up if the right guy came along. Yeah, she had a dangerous side all right! I wasn't about to mess with someone else's girlfriend, so I promptly bailed on the date.

I called Shaun immediately. "Hey idiot, Felicia is still with Darren!"

"I know," he admitted. "I just wanted her to meet you because Darren is a tool, and you're awesome! Felicia's my friend, and you're my best friend, and I just think you two would be a good pair!"

"That may be, but not now at least" I said.

A year passed.

I was busy with my band, she apparently with cosmetology school.

One night, Shaun and I were out on the town with Bailey, and we ran into Felicia, except this time, she looked and acted off, even to Bailey who had known her for years. To make matters even stranger, she had drastically changed her hair. To the point that it was actually a huge turn off. It looked like a bad perm meets something that the band "Flock of Seagulls" would have worn in the 80's, with bleached highlights. It was absolutely hideous. So much so that I actually said out loud, "What in the world happened to your hair"?

"Screw you! I like it., she responded and quickly turned her head.

I tried saving face by asking her about school and whatever else, but she was giving me the cold shoulder. And rightfully so. I had only just made fun of her right to free expression.

A few days later, I was out dancing and I ran into Felicia yet again.

I tried to avoid her, but she walked up to me and in a sassy tone and asked, "Does tonight's hair meet your approval?"

"Yeah actually, vast improvement from a few days ago!" I said.

Looking back on it, I still can't believe how arrogant I was.

Then she fired back, "Well, since it meets your approval, you should dance with me."

So we danced the night away, had some laughs and when I asked about Darren, she said he was history. She slipped her number in my pocket and told me to call her.

The next day, I called her and we made plans to go out a couple of days later. We got dinner, went to her apartment, which was conveniently located above her cosmetology school and across the street from a local strip joint in the downtown area of the city.

A few days after that, Felicia and Bailey reconnected and eventually we all went out together on a Friday night. That's myself, Felicia, Shaun and Bailey, as well as my friend Corey as a fifth wheel. We had a night on the town, no drinking either. We just went bowling and got dinner—typical double date stuff.

At the end of the night, Shaun and Bailey drove separately, so Felicia, Corey and I drove back together in my car.

We dropped Felicia off at her apartment, close to midnight. Corey and I watched her go inside her apartment door and we then drove to my place, Corey's car was parked there.

No more than five minutes later, Felicia calls my cell.

She tells me that Darren jumped out of the bushes after we left and assaulted her; he slammed her hand into her apartment room door and then he pushed her around a bit and tried getting them back together.

First off, what bushes, I wondered. Her apartment doesn't have bushes! She lives downtown; it's a concrete jungle. I let that fact slide though. I figured she was just traumatized. Second, don't call me first! Call the police!

Corey and I headed back over. She let us inside the apartment, and her hand had a large red welt on it. She was shivering, so it was obvious something happened.

This was my first time dealing with the issue of domestic violence. Corey and I immediately agreed that the best thing to do was call the police. We figured, since there were no cameras and it was her word verses his, that at best, she could maybe get a restraining order against Darren.

However, we called the police against Felicia's will, so she was mad and slammed her bedroom door and didn't come out till the police arrived, nor did she want to talk to anyone, especially Corey and I.

The police took statements from all of us , and we were about to leave, when we overheard the cops asking Felicia what her affiliation with Darren was. We were stunned to hear her say, "We were engaged but broke it off a week ago."

Engaged! Come again?

This was news to me.

Corey and I left at about 2 a.m. when the police excused us.

At 5 a.m. Felicia texted me and told me she hated me for what I did to Darren and to never talk to her again. She cussed me out and said some other unkind things.

I should have dropped it and never spoken to her again, but being an arrogant 21 year old at that time, I texted her back, trying to get the last word in and told her that Darren was the one to blame; his actions landed him in hot water. He hit her, not me after all.

A few hours later, I had to work at 10 a.m. on a Saturday at my DJ job.

On my way there, I get a call from Shaun. He had a serious tone:

"Heard you had a wild night after we separated last night," he said seriously. "Well, brace yourself, I've got major news for you." He took a deep breath. "First, the police arrested Darren this morning at his work on domestic violence charges. They had to drag him away; he was kicking and screaming all the way to the police car claiming he didn't do it." He paused. "He told them you did it."

At this point, I freaked out. Did I have to get a lawyer? I didn't do anything but still, what did people do in situations like this?

Then Shaun continued:

"Second, remember how we all thought she was kind of "off" the other night? Well, Bailey reached out to her family, and it turns out, no one has seen much of her over the last year because she has been in/out of rehab and has a serious crystal meth problem. She is still going to cosmetology school, but she is about to flunk out because of missing classes, fueled in part by the drugs." He hesitated. "And oh yeah, the kicker—she's also a stripper! At the joint across the street from her apartment."

I was floored. I unknowingly went out with a meth-head stripper and now trouble was following me!

No sooner did I get into work when the police called me. The investigator told me that Darren was arrested and has made bail now, and that while he was in custody, Darren accused me of hitting Felicia.

I have to hand it to the police, they were nothing but awesome to me. They told me they knew he was lying, that they had solid witnesses to verify my whereabouts all through out the night. I guess in this case, it pays to live with your parents!

The police advised that I not contact Felicia and I agreed. I was already done with her after her rude text that morning!

But it got crazier!

Shaun was at church, rehearsing for the Easter play, when he got interrupted by Darren, who came in and asked him where I was. He told him that he was going to kick my ass for what I did to Felicia. Darren also knew where I worked and told Shaun that he would find me there. So after the conversation ended, Shaun immediately called me to let me know. Needless to say, I was concerned for my safety.

Then my pastor called me, which was not uncommon, since I'm heavily involved at church. He told me that Felicia's parents go to our church, and they'd heard that I recently had gone out with their daughter. Apparently, they got my name from Darren parents, and called my pastor to tell him that their daughter was a habitual liar, off her medication for mental illness issues, and as a result, they were concerned for me because they too doubted that I hit her.

It's pretty bad when your own parents say you're a liar and warn others to stay away, even going out of their way to track me down to inform me of this.

My pastor advised I stay away from her and I couldn't agree more!

Then, it got ugly…

For the next three weeks, Felicia continually tried contacting me. She called and left messages on my home phone, my cell, at both of my jobs… it was uncomfortable. She would start showing up to places I was at to confront me, upset that I wasn't answering her calls …. And to boot, she still wanted to date!

One day, she finally stopped calling.

After that, I never saw her again.

There is much that is unclear in this story, the police (and those of us involved) were able to piece this much together:

Felicia slammed her own hand in the door for attention. She contacted me and Darren the night of the incident, hoping one of us would show up and come to her rescue or that Darren would see her with me and become jealous.

Darren got the charges dropped. She admitted to lying in court; whether she made it all up or did it to protect Darren from further punishment, who knows? Last I heard, she is a mother now and sadly still struggles with addiction.

Lesson learned… it's okay to do a basic background check on someone before going out; otherwise, you never know what you might be stepping into!

Chapter 5
I Once Made Out in the Costco Parking Lot

So far in life, up until this point I've had some relationships that the word "reciprocate" was not present in the women's vocabulary. But with Kelly, it was nice to finally go out with someone who was affectionate with me.

To this day, I'm convinced that Kelly King was the only woman that actually liked me... No seriously, of all the dates and relationships I've had, I think Kelly might have been the only one that genuinely smiled when I did something nice for her and genuinely meant it; she was that appreciative of my kindness to her.

The only problem was... she was too affectionate.

It all started under awkward circumstances, per my usual way I meet someone. As you can tell by now, nothing comes easily for me.

The day before I went out with Jamie, Kelly contacted me on a dating site. Kelly was cute and seemed fun, but here is the thing, I only date one person at a time.

People have different perspectives on this, but I think it's wrong to go out with one person one day and then someone totally different the next and just weed out one or more potential partners eventually till you know what you want. I think you should pick one person, really invest, get to really know them and if they aren't what you feel is right, then move on.

The fact is, sometimes it takes a few dates to really know someone.

So I was honest with Kelly. I told her that I had already agreed to meet Jamie and that I had to say no to a date right now.

Two days later, Kelly checked in:

> ✉ How did things go with that Jamie girl?

I felt kind of awkward talking to her about this and simply replied:

> ✉ Good enough that we are going out again and that once again, I'm sorry but I feel it's wrong for all involved for me to go out with you at this point too. I don't want to play games with anyone's heart here. I wish you the best though.

A month later, I was still with Jamie and Kelly again messaged me and said probably the most attractive thing to me:

> ✉ I just want you to know that I'm getting off this site. All I met were jerks. However, I really wanted to meet you. You seem so genuine in your profile and that is what I am searching for in someone. If you are still seeing Jamie, I wish you the best of luck, but if she is out of the picture or if things one day don't pan out with her, I would really like to know you. Feel free to call me.

She left me her cell number... and I'm not sure why, but I kept it.

I figured that maybe as great as I thought Jamie was, what if things didn't pan out? Kelly seemed like a really awesome person and clearly saw me the same way.

Of course, Jamie broke up with me, and after a couple of days, I decided to dust myself off and try again. I called Kelly and she was still single; so we went out a few days later.

Kelly was from Australia, so she had a really strong accent. That was the first thing that stood out about her to an American like me, but she was very friendly and easy to talk to. We went to this terrible Mexican restaurant but despite the food, I think we were thrilled to be getting to know each other.

I really got the impression that men used and treated her like dirt or like an obligation before me... and it was really too bad, she is such a sweet woman!

I asked her why she wanted to meet me so bad and her honesty also was a big turn on:

"I want to date a guy who lives out his faith and you do" she said firmly. "I want a guy who isn't going to take advantage of me physically. That has been a sin struggle for me in the past and I want a guy that is going to hold me accountable to that. I assume you are a virgin, I am not." I appreciated her honesty and how upfront she was "For someone to be 35 and still a virgin shows that you take that area of your life serious. Few men do nowadays".

Wow! Great answer.

From that point on, we started texting and going out and just being friends with the intention of wanting more.

Kelly was also the first woman to call me just to talk. Actually talk. Not text. Annia despised talking on the phone, and Jamie did it only in an emergency to firm up some information, but never just to hear my voice. You probably don't realize this, but I have a deep, sexy voice. That's how I got my job in radio, actually. Why wouldn't a woman want to hear it? I have always been curious. I always thought that women found men with deep voices attractive, like Barry White and Isaac Hayes. After a long day of work, while lying in bed, Kelly would call just to check in and say hi. It was nice having someone who found comfort in my voice, not just my words via text or email.

Then came Date #4.

We had a great day together. It was beautiful outside, and we went Geocaching for most of the day, which would become a regular activity for us. We just walked and talked and it was a fun day.

Kelly also had another distinction: she was the first woman to want to take her picture with me. She was happy to show other people that she liked standing by my side. I'm an amateur photographer, so I asked to take her picture with the setting sun as the backdrop and she said, "only if you are in it." I was massively turned on. This gal actually likes me!

At this point, this might have been the best date I ever had. It was a perfect day.

As I was dropping her off, I saw sadness in her eyes like I had never seen before, not just from her, but any woman really. When Jamie or Annia showed me sadness, it was because of some pain in their lives. However, Kelly was sad because our day together was ending and I had to drive home. I was taken aback. All the women previous to her just seemed to use me. This woman really liked me. For me. And obviously, I liked her too.

I told her previously that I wouldn't try kissing her till she was ready to go down that road. Just like I offered Annia and Jamie too. They never wanted to take me up on that and in Annia's case, it took months till she finally did. And in Jamie's case, she never did. So at this point, I was used to having to wait to receive affection like this from a woman and again, I didn't mind. All I cared about was knowing Kelly as a person, protecting her heart, and treating her right.

Apparently I was doing a good job, because she was missing me and I hadn't even driven away yet!

I asked her "What's wrong? and with sadness in her eyes she told me "I don't want you to leave" and I felt really valued and I told her "I don't want to go either, but remember, we have some awesome plans ahead for us this upcoming week together and to look forward to sharing those with you."

She then asked the question that all women ask that have more on their minds but are waiting for a chance to unleash:

"What are you thinking right now?"

I told her the truth: "I'm thinking that I really want to kiss you right now." I paused, and then smiled. "Do I have your permission to do that?"

She leaned in and I was planning on giving her a slow, deep first kiss. Much like when I kissed Annia that one time in my life.

Remember, at this point, my "kissing experience" up until then was one night with Annia, which, at this point, had been over a year ago. I felt pretty inadequate or un-trained. I had no idea what I was doing.

So I leaned in, our lips touched for about a second, and then to my shock, she immediately stuck her tongue in my mouth!

This was great!

We were speaking in tongues all right, and it wasn't the same kind the Greens wanted out of me.

Touchdown! Congratulations! You're 35 and just graduated to your first make out session!

I eventually pulled away and nervously asked, "Did I do that right?" (I said the same to Annia).

Kelly laughed and said "Yes, you are a very good kisser. Please kiss me again!"

And so I did. And for the next hour we just sat in my car and made out. Like car windows fogged up. Like Jack-and-Rose-in-*Titanic* type of action!

Then, the catch…

I was totally satisfied with just kissing. I was having a great time. But then she tried to upgrade our make out session to sex… and I was stunned!

Here is the first issue: I have really good self-control. She did not. So after this night, this subject became the crutch in our relationship. Cuddling would lead to kissing and then kissing would make her want more. That is a natural feeling, but without mutual self control, then all will be lost.

I was new to this as well, because she told me up front she didn't want to have sex and obviously neither did I. So, I thought this was our mutual goal. In many ways, I felt bad. I was worried that I was doing something wrong or inappropriate that made her want to go down that route.

I was just coming off my relationship with Jamie, where she said sex was off the table before we ever went out and it was nice to have to not worry about that subject. But now with Kelly, I realized I would.

The next time Kelly and I went out, we had fun as we always did; but now we kissed here and there, too. She was the first gal to hold my hand in public. It was invigorating for me to go to the movies or walk into a restaurant and have her attached to me. She was happy to show everyone that I was special.

Making Kelly happy was easy. Unlike the other women I had been with, every time I did something for her, she thought it was the nicest thing ever. Kelly loves chocolate, so once she told me her favorite brand, and I surprised her with every kind of chocolate that brand offered. That was over $100 in chocolate bars, and she thought that was the sweetest thing ever! Well, it kind of was, literally and figuratively.

Once I surprised her on a snow-covered night when it was literally a blizzard out, with flowers and her favorite coffee. When people were ordered off the roads, I got on them instead, to go be with her I constantly did things like this to make sure she knew I valued her. That particular time, I almost got in an accident—I hit black ice several times and skidded off the road multiple times—but I just had to kiss her.

For the next few weeks, things were great; we would cuddle and kiss and watch the sun set. We would have nice talks, and say and do nice things for each other. Everything was nice.

She even went to a football game with me. Where I come from, going to a Husker football game means you're special! That was a great day. Rugby is practically the national past time in Australia and it's similar to American football, so she had a great time and I didn't mind explaining the differences in our two sports. She taught me about rugby, and I taught her American football. Later that day, we went Geocaching as always, holding hands and kissing. It was such a great day.

Kelly was the first girl to go to the movies with me. She loved going to new restaurants with me; she let me feed her food. She even liked going to the comedy clubs with me. She was fun, and I like to have fun, so we had fun together! When I look back on my time with her, "fun" and "happy" are the first words that come to mind.

With Annia or Jamie, the bad times out weighed the good. When I think about them, I often get sad about what could have been, but with Kelly, things were great for a time.

But then things took a turn for the worse.

One day, we had a nice night together, just like any night; we were cuddling on her couch and that led to kissing and making out as always but this time, as I ran my hands through her long hair, she grabbed them and placed them on her breasts… that's right… boobies. Yeah!

I love breasts. What guy doesn't? And now I was touching some for the first time! Not the accidental-brushing-into-them-while-I-was-dancing like all the years previous, but Kelly wanted me to enjoy hers. Life was great! Then she put her hand in my crotch, and I freaked out. I jumped back, and she said "I'm sorry, it's just so hard to not have sex with you. I really like you. Don't you like me?"

"Of course I like you," I pleaded "but this isn't what I want and neither do you! You told me you liked me because you knew I wouldn't try going that far with you!"

This night was difficult on us both. I had a woman who actually really liked me, so much so that there was no one else in the world she'd rather have sex with than me. Frankly, I was flattered.

Things got worse when she told me that for the upcoming weekend. She wanted to rent a cabin for us. We would share a bed and wood-burning fire and just be together. She showed me the flier for the place we were going stay at and it looked fun, sitting by the fire and talking and kissing, but I knew sleeping in the same bed together would lead to trouble. I offered to get a separate bed, and she got upset. I told her that sleeping in the same bed and spooning would just encourage both of us to cross lines that neither wanted to ultimately cross.

She started to cry. It was a hard talk. I said no because that was what I had committed to God and to myself. No sex till marriage. No sharing beds till marriage. She got upset and said that cuddling on the couch was the same thing as spooning in a bed, and she did have a point. But I still put my foot down.

The next day, I was hanging with Paul and Keith. They both had met Kelly at this point and asked how things were going. I was happy to brag that finally, I had moved up the ladder and now I was touching breasts. Our conversation was about to turn into a high school boys' locker room when Paul put me in my place fast.

"What's the matter with you?" Paul demanded. "First, what are doing? You aren't guaranteed to be spending your life with Kelly, so right now you could be inappropriately touching someone else's wife!" He glared at me. "You need to think about that! Ask yourself, would you have treated Jamie the same way? Would you have ever grabbed her breasts?"

"Well, I probably wouldn't have. I respected her too much." I said.

"Then you need to show that same respect to Kelly as well," Paul responded. "We all know you're a good guy and she knows it too. But now you need to act like it!" I felt a little preached at, but I knew he was right. As a man of God, I needed to show more restraint. But now, I also sympathized with how tempted Kelly must feel: once you cross a line, it's hard to not cross it again.

There was also another catch…

While I liked Kelly and was starting to fall for her, the fact was I was fresh off my relationship with Jamie and when it came to the subject of God, Jamie and I were on the exact same page. Kelly and I were on the same page too, but just not the whole book, per say.

So whenever something would go wrong with Kelly, I'd take it as a sign to keep trying to make it work with Jamie. Now Kelly got all my attention, but that didn't stop me from texting Jamie and putting feelers out there and trying to get her attention. This is also after Jamie's mother told me she wanted Jamie and me to reunite. It was hard to decide what I was supposed to do.

Kelly and I continued to date, and we continued to have fun. We had a healthy relationship for awhile again.

But there was a point when I realized that I was in the wrong.

I like to plan surprise dates, so one night before taking her to dinner and a night at the local comedy club, I surprised her with a trip to Costco. She was always fascinated with America's "bigger is better" mentality, how we have bigger portion sizes of everything, all-you-can-eat-buffets. She thought Costco embodied that, so she mentioned once that she had always wanted a look inside. So I took her to Costco as the first stop on the evening's date, and allotted an hour for her to enjoy all things Costco. She was ecstatic! She loved the little surprises like this that I did for her. The only problem was we needed a membership card to get in; I was unaware of this before we got there, so man, I felt stupid! I had only been in once before several years ago and it was with a friend, so I didn't even think about the stupid membership card.

So there we were in the parking lot of Costco, no access to the building and now with an hour to blow before we had to be at the restaurant. "So, now what?" I said. Without skipping a beat, she grabbed me and we started making out. Apparently the thought of the Costco date was a huge turn on. It was kinda trashy, in broad daylight, us all over each other as people walked by and observed our passion for Costco, but hey, I had a great time.

That night was a blast. After dinner and the comedy club as I took her home, she couldn't keep her hands off me. She made out with me at each stop light, which, of course, we hit like clock work. I couldn't be more thankful for the constant traffic delays! She really liked me!

But after that night, I was becoming worried that our relationship was too focused on the physical.

A few weeks later, on a snowy night, I came by to watch a movie and something was off. I brought her cookies and hot chocolate and was ready for a great night together. She didn't want to kiss or snuggle, and she told me she wanted to break up.

She met someone else and she said that because of the whole physical boundaries thing, that it was too much for her and that somehow I made her feel like less of a person because she wanted to go further than I did. To her, she felt oral sex and mutual masturbation were okay to do, but just not full on sexual intercourse. I disagreed. And we argued about this.

Somehow as well, in a discussion from weeks earlier, apparently I said some comments that made her feel ashamed that she had slept with several different guys before meeting me. I remembered that discussion, and I realized I could have phrased things differently, so I apologized. But it was too late. She was done with me.

I drove home that night consumed with sadness. It ended because of the temptation to do more; it would have constantly consumed us since we weren't on the same page on that subject. It was over because I thought it was what God wanted for both of us, the whole "purity" thing. But I was no angel; I'm sure with all our making out, I led her on or enticed her. So I'm to blame as well for our demise.

In the coming months, she would text me here and there and said hello. After we ended, Kelly changed for the better. I guess she needed to be away from me to really focus on God. Three months after we ended, she sent me an article she read in a magazine. It was about what a woman should expect from a guy in a dating relationship when Christ was the focus. She attached a note that brought tears to my eyes.

> 🖂 Thanks for meeting everyone of these expectations. Thanks for respecting me. Every man I have dated since I have compared to your template. Thank you for your devotion to purity. It's an area of my life that I now take even more seriously. Thank you for being so good to me. I pray that God will bless you with a woman that appreciates all of this about you and more! Your friend, Kelly.

I felt such relief. I had been worried that she would look back on our time together and feel that with all our make out madness, that I treated her poorly or disrespected her in some way.

When I look back on my time with Annia or Jamie, maybe I might have been able to get some closure with them if they would have sent a message similar to what Kelly sent. It would have made me feel so much better, hearing from them that the way I treated them or the things I did for them mattered.

In the end, my heart broke over Kelly. But it wasn't exactly her fault. Just like she made it clear when we were together that I was her guy, it was obvious when she started seeing someone new. She posted pictures of her and the "new guy" online, and it tore me up in a way I never felt with Annia and Jamie, since they dated a new guy every week, or so it seemed. Those guys were replaceable and meaningless, but Kelly's new guy—well, he was for real.

Even worse, they went to Las Vegas together after dating for two months. She had begged me to take her there when we were together, and now she found someone who would. I had said no because I know we would have made mistakes and done things there that were dishonoring to God. Now, I'm not saying she did or didn't do anything that might compromise her new commitment to purity while there with the "new guy", but all I knew was for me and my relationship with her at the time, it was something that I wasn't supposed to do with her. But it didn't make me feel any better about the situation.

My time with Kelly taught me how to have fun with someone with no expectations. The only problem was I failed to show her that. She thought I expected her to give physical affection to me as "payment" if you will in return for my kindness; however, I was enjoying it so much that I was constantly wanting it all the same and I never took that time to really clarify that with her. So I regret that.

Kelly has since moved out of state. We still talk here and there. I think very highly of her, and one day she is going to make an awesome mother and wife. I hope God blesses her with a really special man. Truly. She will always have a special place in my heart.

Chapter 6
Pyramid Scheme Dating

When I was 18, I went out with a girl named Allison. She was conservative and reserved in her demeanor, but super cute, beautiful short blonde hair. I met her at church, so I figured this was already headed on the right track.

Now, my friend Shaun and I have had some crazy, stupid adventures together. This was no exception. Shaun and I were fresh out of High School and were happy to be playing the field. Shaun had just started dating his now wife Bailey, so I needed to catch up. So Allison and I went on a double date with Shaun and Bailey.

We went mini golfing (how stereotypical) and I don't remember much after that, all I remember was the rest of the date involved food, because I subsequently set a new world record in fat that night, when in a two and a half hour time span, I ate a whole XL "Works" pizza from Papa John's Pizza, as well as 4 scoops of ice cream at Baskin Robbins and then 3 bags of microwave popcorn. Now, this should have been the sign that Allison should run for the hills from me, but no, she continued to snuggle with me on the couch later that night. Now, that's a sign a girl likes you right? When you consume enough food that even "Jabba The Hut" would tell you to ease up and the girl still sticks around!

During dinner, or should we say, putting me out to pasture, I asked Allison what she does for work...the only problem is, she couldn't give a straight answer to that question. Because of that, many thoughts ran through my mind, I even at one point thought that maybe she was a stripper or something and she just wasn't ready to reveal that yet? How intriguing I thought!

Now, both Shaun and I were looking for work at the time, so we were interested in whatever it was that she was doing. So Allison gave us a card and invited us to an "informal recruit meeting" with her "boss" at "Lifecore" for 2 days later.

After dinner, I let Shaun pick the movie, which was a big mistake. He chose *Enemy At The Gates,* which is a war movie geared toward the male audience. About half way through, Shaun and Bailey had to take off, it left me and Allison alone which I was thrilled with (lovely Allison, my potential stripper girlfriend). Now, I had never seen the movie, so I had no idea what might be coming up next obviously.

Here the thing with traditional conservative Christian girls, they are typically offended by sexual content in films. Well, I had never seen the film before and coming up was a really awkward sex scene and Allison was visibly uncomfortable after it. I guess she was mad that I didn't "fast forward through the "dirty" part" (that I didn't know was coming up mind you!). Well, the night obviously ended awkwardly. She was upset that I didn't pick a cleaner movie and that I should have known better... based on her negative reaction to the content of the film, I guess that then ruled out the possibility of her being a stripper at least.

Well, now I had to play catch up.

Shaun and I went to the Lifecore "offices", which were located in a few suites of a business district that we were familiar with, in fact, my dentist was also in the same set of buildings, just across the street, so it seemed legit enough.

The thing was though, those "offices" felt off from the start, they were under construction, I felt like Michael Douglas in *The Game* when he first walks into the offices of "Consumer Recreation Services (CRS)"… it had elements of being legit, but something still seemed rushed about it.

When we walked in, the place looked fairly bare bones, there was a desk, chairs and then down the hall there was a conference room with flashing blue, green and red lights with strobes that we could see through the crack of the door and not to mention the pounding techno music that was going on. We were both wearing suits and were unaware that really all we had to do was bring Ecstasy!

We sat down, and watched all these other young, well dressed, business professionals such as us come out of the rave down the hall and then the question marks were now really flying. We asked, "what was going on," and the "secretary" told us they have to "confirm" us before we can meet with "Mr. Anderson", Allison's "boss", then we can enter the conference room.

At various points of our 20 minute wait, a separate group of well dressed hipsters, wearing headsets, who had the demeanor of Nazis, were organizing something and kept talking into those headsets like we didn't exist and I think they even ignored us on several occasions on purpose. Eventually, a S.S. headset lady approached us with a neon clipboard with a list of names on it, we were annoyed and ready to leave, but she asked us for our names and said we weren't on the list and eventually another sexy Gestapo lady approached us with another neon colored clipboard and asked us our names yet again and wrote them down on the list, right in front of our faces and then proclaimed "Oh, there you guys are, sorry for the delay, you may enter now." Are you kidding me? Did she not think we saw that!

When we got in there, the room was filed with these business minded people with name tags and were sipping beer from red cups, which I'm nearly convinced was actually filled with Jim Jones flavored Kool-Aid!

As we were just getting settled in at this apparent business rave, a familiar face walked in, a guy named "Pete" that I knew from around the way. Pete is a strange guy, not someone I hang with, just someone I know through various life encounters. He was short of breath and carrying a gym bag, filled to the brim with some devices that I couldn't make out what they were because the gym bag was zipped up, but they looked like they were about the size of a brick and made of plastic by the way they were all just rattling around in the gym bag. Pete was way under dressed, wearing a beer stained striped polo shirt and jean shorts. I thought to myself, who the Hell let this guy in? Then I remembered, it was the same idiots that wrote Shaun and my names down on a clipboard check list, right in front of our faces, like we were already on there the whole time!

Eventually, through the thundering techno music and light show, Allison appeared.

"Did you guys make it in all right?" she wondered.

"Yeah, no prob" (lying of course) I responded.

Just as we were about to start a real conversation with Allison, a guy who clearly had a "leader" vibe of the group announced by shouting, "Hey everyone, take a seat, Geoffrey is about come in!" The lights came up, the music dimmed and then switched to some earthy yoga based music.

Then in walks Geoffrey M. Anderson. He was wearing pinstriped black pants, partially unbuttoned scarlet red shirt, popped collar, with thick rimless glass. He looked like a modernized version of the classic "Saturday Night Live" character "Matt Foley." Except, I truly believe this guy was locked in a basement with a pot of coffee, lines of cocaine, speed and had probably been popping uppers since that morning in 5 minute intervals, all while washing it down with Red Bulls. He is wired! Energetic to the point of annoyance. I'm actually more shocked that his heart didn't explode right there as he hit the stage!

Allison, with all the excitement in the world and beaming eyes said to Shaun and I, "He's here!"...you would have thought that this was the movie *Ghostbusters* and Allison had just outted herself as a "Gozer" worshipper!

Mr. Anderson's voice was on level 11 (His amp didn't stop at 10) at all times, he was shouting, talking fast, moving all around the place and he talked in broad, non specific terms about building a business, about having great personal relationships with your coworkers and your clients and about changing the world through this business and through it's practices... and how might this be accomplished you might be asking?

...water purifiers of course!

Pete, who was sitting at the end of the isle we were in, pulled out his gym bag from beneath his chair and started pulling out these water purifiers with a big old smile on his face, pivoting his body and lifting them in the air for the whole room to see. He looked like "Mola Ram" holding up one of the sacred stones from *Indiana Jones and The Temple of Doom*!

After this, Shaun and I realized that we had been here an hour too long already. Geoffrey continued to speak, and it was clear, that several of the members of Lifecore were planted strategically in the audience. When Geoffrey would say something motivational, someone with a Lifecore name tag would say "Yes Geoffrey" or "Right on" or "I agree!" It was so clearly staged, it was sickening. Finally, Geoffrey announced that they were gonna take a 15 minute intermission (probably so he could mainline some Redbull) and then he was going to return to "workshop" some ideas.

Shaun and I now had a shot at escaping, however we were surrounded by these Lifecore trolls, then Allison signaled someone from across the room and 6 really attractive women walked up, with beady eyes, they looked like extras from the movie *The Stepford Wives*. They approached us and started talking about some earth centered nonsense. Before we knew it, the 15 minutes were up and we were stuck in our seats again.

Mr. Geoffrey M. Anderson then went into another speech about more nonsense and then talked about how he started this "company" and told this elaborate story about, I swear I'm not making this up, about how a bird crapped on his face as he was driving his cherry red sports car and then he heard the voice of God, telling him what he was to do with his life and this business. He was teary eyed as he was telling this story and then in typical Ryan and Shaun fashion, we burst out laughing, we couldn't take another second more of this! Our laughter was soon silenced however by the evil glares from the Lifecore followers that turned around and stared at us.

Geoffrey then explained over and over that this business is "not a pyramid scheme" but instead a "multi level marketing business venture" or "MLM" for short. In English, they are one in the same. Shaun leaned over and said, "I don't care how stupid I am about to look, I'm walking outta here in 2 minutes, with or without you! I don't care how hot Allison may be either, she is not worth your soul!"

Then Geoffrey made everyone stand and put there hands in the air and recite some pledge, which turned into a chant! Then Shaun and I started shouting "LIFE-CORE" over and over with the rest of the crowd, we got up and started high fiving people, just like some of the strategically placed trolls were already doing and then we made a b-line for the door. We were liberated and made it out alive!

I don't know who didn't call who when it comes to Allison and I, but 3 weeks later I saw her at church, fully attached at the hip to some guy who is probably a level 5 Platinum elite member of her MLM/cult and she told me they were getting married and that was it. I don't know what happened to her, I just hope they didn't have to sacrifice their first born!

I'm curious to know if their wedding cake had a water purifier on top of it? At least maybe the groom's cake was in the shape of one perhaps?

Chapter 7
The One Who Got Away?

I have these things I call "dry spells." I'm not the kind of guy that can walk into a room, tell some jokes or share some witty banter and at the end of night, stand at the door of the bar and just collect a bunch of numbers from all the girls I just impressed.

I'm a tough sell, I admit it. I will go months without talking to a woman sometimes.

After Kelly and I ended, I didn't talk to a single, available woman for three months. It wasn't like I didn't try either, I messaged a few, but no one was interested… so not interested in fact that they couldn't write back with a polite rejection.

Then I bumped into Lauren.

I saw her a year ago on a dating site. She seemed awesome of course, so I messaged her and no response. Again, I was used to this. So now a year had passed, and I saw her on a new dating site. This one had a more detailed algorithm and matching system: we were an 88% match, so I was curious as to where that other 12% went.

I compared our answers, and we were a miss on sex. She felt it was ok to have sex before marriage and I didn't. This frankly pissed me off! She and I were a match on everything else important, except for our view on that one subject. She also had a relationship with God, an apparently healthy one too based on her other answers, so her free participation in pre-marital sex concerned me and angered me.

Now, I was just coming off my relationship with Kelly; she'd had a relationship with God too, but to her also, sex was okay, despite what God said in the Bible about it! Maybe that's why I got so bothered by it.

Lauren was a highly educated woman. She was a psychologist.

I'm not sure what came over me, maybe frustration and rage against a secular society and it's influence on other's faiths and moral standards, who knows? But I wrote her my thoughts:

> 🖂 "I'm not trying to score a date by contacting you. You've already rejected me in the past on another site. But I just have to ask—you are clearly a highly educated woman, smart and articulate, so I was hoping you could explain to me your reasoning as to why you think its okay to have sex before marriage? You already know the Bible's view on it, and I assume your church tells you it's wrong as well, so why do you choose to go against that? Now, keep in mind, I agree with what Jesus says in the book of Matthew, that "all sins are equal in the eyes of God." But some sins carry greater emotional ramifications with them, sex being one of the bigger ones. So, knowing this, why then do you feel it's okay to not follow what God has asked of us?"

She could have blocked me after that. She could have not responded at all… but for some reason, she did.

She wrote back her reasons and over the next two weeks over email, we got into this huge dialogue. Lauren was exactly what I thought she might be. She was smart, articulate and highly intelligent. We talked about sex, morals, religion—all kinds of deep things. It was a great two weeks of conversation between two mature adults.

The conversation eventually came to an end and that was that… or so I thought.

Two weeks later, she contacted me on the dating site again and struck up a new conversation. We exchanged new pleasantries and had another good dialogue that lasted another week.

Then I recognized her on Facebook one day and noticed that she was going to see a mutual friend's band play at some local dive bar. So I mentioned this to her and that I was thinking of going. She said we should go together, and I agreed. I had to meet this woman, despite our opposing view on sex (much like Kelly). She had an over-abundance of other qualities to her personality that I thought would drown that subject out.

As I was setting up this encounter, I felt something come over me, almost a voice saying, "This will only lead to heartache. Why would you put yourself through it?"

I couldn't tell if this was just my own doubts trying to talk me out of it, or God trying to get me to pull the plug before things got started?

Either way, I ignored the voice, and we met up.

It's hard to not sound cliché, but it was love at first sight for me. From the instant she walked up to me and said "Hey," I felt comfortable like I had with no other woman.

Lauren had Annia's sense of adventure, wit, intelligence and humor; Jamie's poise and kindness and Kelly's overwhelming happiness. Lauren was the best of all worlds.

I had never met a woman who was cool with going to a concert and just kicking it… but Lauren was and I was thrilled! I was already imagining taking her to see my favorite band Dream Theater. I guessed that she probably wouldn't like them, but she was smart enough to appreciate their musicianship and all the work that goes into what they do. And then we would have a long conversation about it. Lauren was a lot of things, but shallow was not one of them. After that first time hanging out, I could see it all unfolding before me. It could happen, I thought! A woman finally coming to a Dream Theater concert with me, instead of me, alone. Like always.

So we went and saw this mediocre local band, watched people get drunk, made fun of them and just hung out and talked. She was a very open person. On the date, I asked her what her worst date of all time was, and she told me a story about how on an overnight date with some guy, she clogged his toilet… I couldn't believe she shared this! It was hilarious, but most gals wouldn't share something like this, at least not on a first date. After the show, we went to her car and we just talked for a couple hours. It was awesome. And then, when I looked in the back of her car, and saw it was loaded with board games, my heart was hers for the taking. I'm honestly and completely content spending a night playing cards and board games with friends. It's all about the people you play with, the conversations and the friendly competition. Lauren was in the same boat. I couldn't believe this. I potentially had someone to play games with now. Good games, not games with my heart for once!

From that day on, there was only one person in the whole world I wanted to talk to or be with: Lauren. I could say anything, share any idea or perspective on any subject, and it wasn't nonsense to her. She was one of those "The only bad ideas are the ones not shared" types.

During that month, I always had someone to talk to. Lauren was constantly texting me the same kinds of positive affirmations that I sent her; she really saw me—my heart—and appreciated just who I was. I never felt like I had to change anything to impress her. One of the things that made Lauren stand out was that the dialogue never stopped. Whether we were on the phone for hours or talking face to face, there was always more to be explored, more to discuss, more to debate. It was healthy. It was safe. It was fun.

We saw each other at least once or twice a week. Dating Lauren was easy because I didn't have to make all the dramatic overtures that I'd made with girls in the past. Some nights we would just hang out on her couch and talk, and it was the best experience ever. I felt a deeper connection with her than I had ever had with anyone else, and it seemed so easy. My friends were excited too because they have again, lived through all my missteps with women up to that point. They just wanted me to be happy, and it seemed like I had finally found someone that perfectly complimented me. Every single one of my friends agreed.

On the days I couldn't see her, due to her work schedule, I always longed for her late night text that said two simple words:

> 🖂 Still up?

Because if I responded, I knew she would immediately call me and we would talk for hours! I would often talk her to sleep. It made me feel special that as her day ended, it was my voice that she wanted to be sure to hear from last.

Then as soon as it began, it ended.

Out of no where, she texted me.

> 🖂 Hey, I don't have time to talk to night. In fact, I have to be honest. I just don't have feelings for you anymore.

I was crushed.

Crushed in a whole new way. It wasn't like getting dumped in the past. I saw the red flags with the women of my past, so while the endings still hurt with them, it wasn't like with Lauren. I couldn't find something overly wrong with her, or wrong enough that I felt I shouldn't pour every ounce of myself into pursuing her.

I've always had this belief that the relationships in my past ended because God has something better for me. When I met Lauren, I was sure she was that "better." I literally never had a single thought about the women that came before her. All the "what if's" with them immediately went away after my first date with her.

After she cut me loose, I sat down that night and literally stayed up all night and wrote the most passionate letter I've ever written. I told her why she was the most amazing woman on the planet and begged her to give me a second chance.

She wrote back a few days later, giving her reasons why she wanted out; she was direct on some issues and vague on others. Since she was a psychologist, I couldn't tell if she was talking to me like a boyfriend or a patient.

I responded to that email with another longer letter. I poured everything into that yet again.

If she wanted a man who would fight for her, I made it clear that I would in that letter.

But instead, she read it and never responded.

Her silence was the worst.

Three weeks later, she emailed me a link and some questions about a close friend's restaurant. I was shocked. I responded to her questions, but then silence again.

I called my friend Jake; he and his wife Emily had played cards with us before, and he knew how deep my feelings ran for her. Jake also works with her, and I asked if he knew anything about what was going on. He said he knew about our breakup because she brought it up in a discussion and said it was just "too much, too fast." According to him, she still wanted to be friends, maybe even more one day, and that is why she reached out to me again.

The next week, I sent her a link to a restaurant my friends also owned and encouraged her to go.

A week later, on a work night, at 12:30 a.m., she texted me:

.

🖂 Still up?

Now, I usually don't go to bed till 2 a.m., so this wasn't weird, but she usually works out at 5 a.m., so I wondered what was going on.

She called just to talk… so we talked and talked about nothing special, just whatever came to mind. This was all I ever wanted out of life—to talk to this woman. If one day I got to kiss her, even better, but for now, I was happy with just what I had with her.

Of course, I called Melissa the next morning. She was thrilled to hear that Lauren was making contact again.

"Clearly you made an impression!" she said enthusiastically. "She's drawn to your character, and she knows you're worth investing in." She cautioned me to be careful. "Slow and steady wins this race, Ryan. Just hang in there!" Melissa had met Lauren right when we first started dating—I made sure of that! She had approved of Lauren from the get go, and thought she was perfect for me. So her encouragement meant a lot.

So after that, though I was in the usual friend zone, I was determined to get back into the boyfriend zone. Based on Melissa's observations, unlike Annia and Jamie, all I had to do was keep being me and she would come around. I just had to keep being so irresistibly good to her like I was before and so I did.

I took the approach that dating Lauren was like a marathon, and I was willing to run next to her for as long as it took. We talked every night again, and sent each other random texts during the day. Life was good again. I thought maybe she was starting to move past friendship and back toward being interested in me.

As I said before, I'm slow out the gate. Due to a lack of positive experiences, I don't know what to say to really steal a girl's heart. I just speak from mine and on a rare occasion, they react positively.

Lauren made my life even better soon after that when she asked to come to church with me. We went together and out to lunch after and we just sat and talked about the message and our thoughts and how it related to our lives and our current societal landscape. That day was a perfect picture of what I want out of life: the two of us together, bonding, connecting over the simple things, like a message at church or a meal. While there's a part of me that would have loved for some physical affection to be a part of that perfect day, it really was secondary to just being in her presence.

Later that night we went to the local comedy club and eventually got sushi. It was an ideal way to end what had already been the perfect day. On the drive home, she made up songs about random observations that we encountered as we drove and I sang with her; we got silly together and it was just good fun. Her creativity was one more of her many attractive qualities. I couldn't wait for another night like this.

At this point, I could say that I loved Annia for what she could have been. Jamie…well, I fell in love with one version of her that only I got to see on occasion. Kelly, I loved because she was fun but lacked the substance required to sustain a relationship for the long term. But Lauren, she had it all. As the saying goes, "You can't just love some parts of someone, you have to love all of them" And that was exactly how I felt about Lauren.

I fell in love with Lauren for the right reasons. Physically, she was beautiful, so I'm not going to deny or discount that, but I was in love with her as a person. I couldn't wait to talk to her each day. I expected nothing from her when I was with her, I just felt blessed and fortunate that I got to spend time with her. She redefined what a woman should be in my mind.

She was just like me, a perfectly broken person. She had a lot of growing to do in her faith, but so did I. Just in different areas. But for some reason that remained a mystery to both of us, she never felt like she could commit her whole self to me. It was easy for me—I loved her from the minute I saw her. But there was something inside her that wouldn't let go of whatever her reservations were and be mine completely. I would never be able to elevate myself from the friend-zone, and eventually we stopped talking.

As selfish as this sounds, the other hard truth I had to learn was the reality behind the saying, "If you truly love someone, you have to be willing to set them free."

Lauren kept growing closer to God; she kept going to church too… just not with me. She has a very magnetic personality that people are drawn to. She is constantly learning or obsessed with learning, so she is always meeting new people, trying to understand what makes them tick. Because of that, she quickly makes new friends wherever she goes. She eventually stopped sitting with me at church, and instead she started sitting with hipper, shinier people. Ones that wouldn't give me the time of day and that honestly, I probably wouldn't get along with either.

But I grew to hate myself in the process because I had always thought I was smart and intelligent, someone she was attracted to and kept her interest, well rounded, and open… but it seemed like she thought these new friends had more to offer than me. And that didn't make sense in my mind.

Soon I'd spot her at church alone with guys and jealousy started to set in.

The late night phone calls stopped.

Hang outs disappeared and so did she.

At one point, before it all ended, we hung out at her apartment and spent the night just talking as always and twice in the conversation, she just randomly brought up why she didn't want to date me right then. It was like she said it because she was mad at me for not living up to the standard she wanted in a man, because apparently I was close to it, but just not quite there. I'd like to think that she wanted it to happen just as much as me, but it is hard to say. I only have myself to be mad at though, because I'm sure I missed some signs. I could have listened better. I could have communicated better. There are always things I could have done better. But it was too late. I lost her.

It still breaks my heart when I think back to the last time I spoke to Lauren. We talked on the phone for three hours. At times the silence was so strong you could hear a pin drop on either side. We got into a heated discussion about why we couldn't be in a relationship; more so, that I wanted one with her and she didn't with me. I told her the truth, that I really loved her and for the right reasons and she agreed that my motives in my feelings for her were pure, but she was frustrated that she just couldn't develop those same feelings for me. She was mad because she knew we couldn't be friends, that my love for her would overshadow every conversation we'd have and that she would always have her guard up in those future conversations because of my deep feelings for her. That night when I hung up the phone, I knew "goodnight" was really "goodbye".

I go to a church that averages close to 3,000 a service. So it's easy to get lost in the crowd. But somehow, if I look, I always find her. She's there with other men, or other people. Sometimes it still hurts so bad that I've walked out of church because I just get that distracted and mad at myself for not showing her the man that I know I am. I feel like if I could have shown that to her, she would have never left.

We don't speak anymore. Part of that is my fault. It would be just too hard watching her move on with someone else close up and in my face; I couldn't handle hearing her talk about being with anyone else.

I could never be truly happy for her with some other guy because I still believe that we bring out the best in each other. She makes me the best version of myself. That is what makes being friends impossible for us. Maybe she knows I'm in love with her and the psychologist in her says "stay away".

For whatever man finally wins her heart… congratulations! Expect your tires to be slashed on a weekly basis. You've won the gift of a lifetime, and I doubt you have any idea!

Fact is, Lauren knew me better than I knew myself. Because of that, maybe she saw something negative in me that I still can't see or fully grasp, and she was just avoiding potential mutual heartache down the road. I don't think I will ever fully understand or know.

They say you should want to marry your best friend, and that is who I lost. This was the woman who once called me up and talked on the phone for two hours strictly to play through a "mad gab" book with me. She was the woman that if I had made us watch "The Karate Kid 1 & 2" while eating Chinese food for a date, she would have thought that was the coolest thing ever (that is still my ultimate fantasy date by the way). Lauren liked me for me and when I was around her, I feared nothing. She made me feel like I was invincible, that I mattered. The only thing I feared was losing her… and I did.

To sum up my experience with Lauren, a quote from the late Rich Mullins comes to mind: "My wife is married to someone else. I'm convinced that is what God had to do, to get me to solely focus on him."

Now, I'm not saying that I will never meet anyone else. God can do anything! But based on my experiences thus far, I doubt it. All I can do is focus on God, and if the female void is something he chooses to fill with some awesome gal, then I welcome it! But if not, I have to continue to struggle to find contentment. Because for me, contentment in my singleness just might be a lifelong battle.

Lauren was my first real, healthy relationship. I learned a lot, but the big take away was to embrace diversity. Though we saw eye to eye on a lot of things, and that is what constantly kept the fires burning in our conversations, when it came to what would have normally been a deal breaker for me, I didn't write her off like I would have with other people. I got to know everything else about her. Though we didn't see eye to eye at the time on premarital sex, I ultimately knew that I likely wasn't going to budge. Remember, I just dated Kelly, and she wanted to go down that road more than once. I constantly turned her down. I have a lot of will power. After all, I'm the guy who is 35 and still hasn't had a sip of alcohol. The more time we spent together and the more she started going to church and growing in her own personal journey with God, the more I saw that "deal breaker" was no longer going to be an issue. The only problem is that we grew apart in other ways. I fell deeper in love with her each day, and she just didn't see me the same way. Because I really got to know her, I can honestly say I lost a true companion, something I've never had with any other woman.

That is why I miss her. I miss her more than any words could possibly convey.

And I won't lie.

Sometimes I stay up later than I should and I always leave my phone on… hoping tonight will be the night she texts me again and asks me the question I would love to hear…

🖂 Still up?

Chapter 8
Ninja Date #1

For those of you who are unaware, a "ninja date" or at least as it's been described to me, is when you get together with someone with the intent on friendship, but the other person has other intentions.

I have been the recipient of this before. Here a classic one for you:

At some point in my early 20's, my friend Robert had just started dating his now wife Shelly. They lived two states away and met through online dating, which was a new thing at the time. This was only the 2nd time in three months that Robert was going to be spending actual face to face time with her. She was coming to spend the weekend with him, and this was a pretty big deal to him obviously.

At the time, Robert was living with his ultra-plutonic friend Ja'Quaelah. They used to work together and became pals ever since; they shared a two-bedroom apartment with "Mr. Scraps" and "Cleo", her two damn cats.

Now, I'm not trying to make issue of this, but just so you get a full picture of Ja'Quaelah, she is African American, full bodied, very forward, and loud.

I'd ran into Ja'Quaelah on a few occasions obviously because of my friendship with Robert. She also went to the same church as us, so she was someone we'd see around and converse with. I have no issue with her otherwise; she is a nice person, always laughing at something and finding humor in everything.

So one night, Robert called and told me that Shelly was coming for the weekend and he wanted me to meet her. So he set things up that we were going to dinner and then a movie.

Now, I thought this was kind of weird from the start… this was only the second time he was hanging out with Shelly and he was already introducing her to friends? For me, if it's that early on in a relationship and I got my girlfriend on a weekend pass, I'd be hogging her all to myself! I wouldn't want anyone enjoying my time with her, but apparently Robert thought differently.

My car was in the shop that week, so Robert picked me up. First mistake.

We showed up to the restaurant, and there was this Shelly he had been talking about endlessly. And then Ja'Quaelah was there too. This was unannounced, but whatever. Again, I didn't really know her well, so this gave me a chance to have someone else to talk to other than my napkin when Robert/Shelly were having a moment together. I thought maybe even Robert invited Ja'Quaelah so I wouldn't feel like a 3rd wheel. I was wrong.

So we sat down in this large booth with Ja'Quaelah next to me… and from the start, Ja'Quaelah started brushing up against my thigh. Now, there was plenty of room, but she kept saying, "Excuse me" or "Sorry about that!" But it wasn't like she was hard of hearing and had to constantly lean in; the restaurant was plenty quiet! It was obviously intentional.

As the dinner conversation continued, Ja'Quaelah kept laughing at everything I said. Like, even the stuff that I didn't intend on being funny and that I knew wasn't funny.

As dinner ended, we were actually going to go bowling, but settled on the movie, which I knew was going to be a problem because at the time, there wasn't really anything worth seeing in the theatres and I'm picky. So while I would have jumped at a horror film without thinking twice, I had to remember that I was with a group of people that find "Veggie Tales" entertaining.

We settle on the suspense/thriller *Identity*. Second mistake.

On the way there, Shelly pulled Robert aside and told him that she didn't want to see the film and nor should he, because it was rated "R" and that Christians shouldn't purposefully expose ourselves to "rated R" content." This message got relayed to me via Robert when we got to the theatre.

Now I was annoyed because everyone agreed at dinner this was the best movie option for the night, but somehow in the two minutes it took to walk from the parked car in the theatre's lot to the front door, Shelly was able to communicate to Robert that we were all hell bound if we watched this!

Honestly, I thought she just wanted alone time finally with Robert, and I couldn't blame her. She only traveled several hours for a whole weekend with Robert, and frankly I still didn't know what I was doing there with them!

Then Ja'Quaelah chimed in. "Ya'll do what ya want—me and Ryan are going to see this here movie and we're gonna get our suspense on!" Suddenly, for that fleeting moment, Ja'Quaelah's cool points rose.

So Robert and Shelly went for a walk and said they would pick us up in two hours, like they were our parents or something (it really felt that way after the "rated "R" talk). But they did drive after all.

Ja'Quaelah and I went to the snack bar and got a big bucket of popcorn. Mistake #3.

We sat down, I put the arm bar/divider down between our two seats and she immediately pulled it up. I put it down again, and she again pulled it up and said, "Can't you see? I'm a big girl. Stop fiddling with this divider non-sense!" She had plenty of room but was faking it. I should have gotten up right then and sat a seat apart or something, but she probably would have followed. So I went along with it. Mistake #4.

As the movie went on, Ja'Quaelah was loud and obnoxious! She threw popcorn at the screen at various times and spoke out, rather loudly, of her disproval of various plot points.

The icing on the cake was when a character died, and one of the others started to express sympathy for this. She loudly said, "Aw, hell no! That dumbass bitch deserved to get her ass stabbed!" I was so embarrassed; my face was firmly hidden within my hands at this point, hoping that even in the dark of the theatre, no one would recognize me.

During the whole film, she kept rubbing her shoulder against mine, like one of her damn cats might rub a scratching post. It was uncomfortable. She kept saying, "Hold me, I'm scared!" I happily resisted. She even tried rubbing my leg at one point.

It was obvious she wanted to be more than friends, and I wasn't interested at all.

When the movie ended (which wasn't soon enough I might add—it had a bad twist ending), Ja'Quaelah announced that the movie sucked because of the ending and that I "owed her a new film." I joked my way around it, but by the time we got outside the theatre and saw Robert and Shelly waiting, she again stated her case to them. Robert and Shelly agreed a more appropriate film would be a good idea.

Again, I didn't drive... so I was at Robert's mercy. Because I didn't want to walk the ten miles home, I went along with the new plan... another movie. This time we went to a local video store (remember those?) and we got the foreign film *Life is Beautiful*, a nice heart-warming film about a Jewish man trying to use humor and entertainment to save his family from the Nazis. Mistake #5.

So we got back to Robert and Ja'Quaelah's apartment, put the movie in and just as we were about to start, Robert asked if I wanted popcorn. I took him up on the offer, since Ja'Quaelah had thrown all of mine at the movie screen when we were at the theatre I was still craving some. Shelly followed him into the kitchen, and they were gone for about ten minutes. He eventually emerged with a giant bowl of popcorn and said, "Just start the movie without us. We're going for a quick walk."

Oh great! Now, once again I was stuck watching a movie with Ja'Quaelah, while Robert and Shelly tried to walk off their sexual urges.

Meanwhile, I was sitting on a loveseat chair and Ja'Quaelah was on the couch. She started petting one of the open seat cushions and said, "You know, there is plenty of room on this couch…"

"Um. I'm good," I responded.

But then, out of nowhere, one of her damn cats made a weird purring noise. It was awkward. Ja'Quaelah then explained that Cleo the cat had an artificial wind pipe or something, so that was why the cat made that strange noise when it purred. Cleo should have its name changed to "Regan" from *The Exorcist* because Hellcat—as I started calling him—was freaking me out at this point!

Then Ja'Quaelah said, "Don't mind the cat. Why don't you come over here and make this kitty purr?" I nervously laughed and tried to pretend I didn't know what she meant.

She kept calling me "Cutie" too, which weirded me out.

During the movie, all she did was complain because it had subtitles. She would say, "Hey cutie, why don't you come over here and read those subtitles to me?"

SOMEONE SAVE ME!

When the movie was over, I couldn't leave fast enough. But that wasn't until I was able to track down Robert, who was "walking" with Shelly in the middle of night.

On the drive home, Robert said "So what do you think of Ja'Quaelah? She has a crush on you, ya know?"

Yeah… I know!

Chapter 9
And All I Got Was a Foot Massager

How do you explain the unexplainable?

Take a black hole for instance. We know they exist, but because no one has been close enough to one, we have no idea what they really are or what they really do in the grand scheme of things in the universe. We have an idea of how they were created, but that's about it.

My time spent with Elisha was much the same.

It's clear by now that Lauren got a bigger part of my heart than anyone before her. She was the first woman who I deeply connected with. She was the first person to really vocally appreciate me for who I was and not what I had to offer.

I fell in love with her for the right reasons, but one of those reasons, I don't think even she really understood.

Toward the end of my time with her, a big life event happened. I got fired from my job in medical records, which I had for seventeen years. Adding to that, I was ousted in dramatic fashion from a camp I had volunteered at each summer for the last seventeen years as well. Both ended because of personal problems with individuals in leadership. While I made mistakes in the process of those working relationships, neither should have ended the way they did. So, two places that were familiar to me and were part of my identity to some degree, were now gone.

Lauren however, unlike many, was able to come alongside me and comfort me during this difficult life transition period. But as I said before, she wanted to only be friends, nothing more, and that's what killed us and eventually resulted in us never talking again.

When you are a man, you want to be a protector, a provider. So, when your financial backing is gone and all you want to do is work but you can't find a steady job, you start to doubt yourself, who you are, what you are capable of. You start to feel like less of a man… but at the time, Lauren, the one I loved still thought I had potential and believed in me. No matter what crappy side job I had to do each day, I knew I'd get to talk to her when it was all over and that she would be proud of me for not giving up.

Now, let talk science again… while we know to some degree what a black hole is, a "wormhole" is different. Scientists believe that if time travel exists, that a wormhole must as well, to transport people at the speed of light to somewhere for a period of time while returning them to the present without time accelerating.

With that being said, I must have been transported through a wormhole to some parallel universe when Elisha came into my life.

It all started like this…

After Lauren and I ended, I joined a new dating site. A few weeks later… guess who also joined? You guessed it. Lauren did as well. I was crushed. A flood of feelings went through me. Then the next day, I got an email from the site that said:

> ✉ Congratulations! Based on all the potential matches available on our site, we have selected one that we know will best fit you! Like you, she is a Christian, she is adventuresome, an extrovert, loves board games and according to our test results, like you she is articulate, creative and intelligent.

...and guess who they picked... yup, Lauren!

I actually started crying, because I was still in love with Lauren. But I knew she would never love me. So I had to move forward and thought I could, but seeing her again and knowing other men were going to be lusting after someone I respected so deeply angered me!

But Lauren said it herself: "If you love me, than you'll be willing to set me free and if I return, than you'll know God put it on my heart."

And since she was out there clearly looking for other men, I had every right to try to find another woman as well.

When I saw Elisha's profile, she seemed like a really delightful person. Clearly artistic, articulate, intelligent and attractive to boot, so I messaged her. Apparently, I gave off the same vibe, so we started emailing each other for a few days.

Elisha was a traveling nurse. She had a three month assignment in central Nebraska, which she was nearing the end of, I came to find out.

I asked her the same question over email that I do on most first dates:

> 🖂 Tell me something about yourself that I wouldn't think to ask.

Some women answer that with a silly answer, like saying they hate some type of food, but the question is meant to encourage them to address serious stuff in a casual manner, like if she has diabetes or missing a limb or something.

Elisha told me she hated sushi. That was her answer. Kinda pissed me off actually, but she told me she liked the question itself and redirected it back to me.

At this point, my life was in upheaval and of the many things I learned from being with Lauren, it was this: if a woman doesn't like me for me, at any given moment, than she isn't worth my time. Lauren didn't care that I was broke and unemployed; she just wanted to talk to me. Lauren told me, "You have a heart of gold and that is your defining characteristic."

So when Elisha asked my question back, I responded this way:

> 🖂 I'm a 35 year old virgin who lives with his parents and is un-employed. While I could give you a good and honorable explanation for my current life circumstances, for some, it might just be too much to handle. If you are willing to look past this, just as you have asked me to do with you leaving in a month and going into a relationship with someone who'll be gone, than let me take you out tomorrow, otherwise, I

wish you the best of luck in your
continued search to find someone
special.

She responded simply:

🖂 See you tomorrow!

And just like that I entered the parallel universe.

The next day I drove to meet her in the middle of Nebraska where she was working at some typical small town hospital.

Our first date lasted twelve hours.

All we did was talk. It was kind of insane when you really think about it. I picked her up, and we went for a long walk around this lake, and we just kept walking and talking, walking and talking, walking… and… talking!

The conversation never stopped.

We had just about everything in common: God, beliefs, morals. She was nearly as big a movie buff as me! We liked a lot of the same bands and the ones we didn't match up on, she wanted to hear. She believed in the same conspiracy theories that I was into. The similarities didn't stop. She even loved card and board games. Who was this person? And why hadn't I met her sooner? It was like I was talking to a female version of myself.

We were nearly the same age; she was European by birth but had lived in the U.S. for the last ten years. She had all kinds of unique things about her: she was a talented painter and writer. She was even working on a screen play because like me, she thinks Christian movies like *Fireproof* and *Facing the Giants* are kind of hokey. She wanted to make a movie with Christian undertones that didn't make believers look like "moral mutants," as we joked… flat out, Elisha was awesome at this point!

Later in the day, we took a paddle boat on the lake.

As we kept talking, she started making future dates for us. Granted we had been talking for a few hours and were clearly connecting, but she really liked me. I was kind of taken aback. I had forgotten what that feeling was like.

She really tripped me out when we sat down afterward on a bench for a few more hours to talk and said, "I don't get it. You love Jesus, you're hilarious, intelligent, thoughtful and handsome. Why again are you single?"

I ignored all the other observations and compliments she just made and responded, "You think I'm handsome"?

Fact was, no one before her had ever said that to me. Not even Lauren… and I love her! They may have thought that, but they never complimented me on my physical appearance. And after all, Jamie once said all the same compliments about me too, but that I was physically repulsive in so many words, so I couldn't tell if this was a sick game or something.

I told Elisha that I didn't know how to take that compliment after what Jamie said about me. I also answered her question by telling her about my relationships and experiences with Annia, Jamie and Kelly. She was stunned by my lack of positive relationships, but also told me that she was in the same boat and felt like less of a mutant knowing that good guys like me still existed.

She told me she thought she was cursed, that the longest any guy had lasted was five dates... more on that later.

I asked her, "Why me though?" Beyond the compliments she had just paid me, because it seemed to me like she could have had her pick of the litter on any given day when it comes to men.

Before she even answered, I realized something. She liked me because I was projecting that I liked myself. Lauren had enjoyed my company, but something on her end was holding her back and that wasn't my problem. Now it looked like Elisha wanted to move ahead, and I knew I should go for it full force.

She said, "Your stock is rising, while I'm sure most women would write you off because of your current life situation, I see way more in you! You have an absolute heart of gold! From your charity and volunteer work, to the way you have treated me just in these first few hours together, it's clear you live out your faith but you aren't a mutant in the process! Above that, like you, I am also a virgin and I know that you will always respect my body while we are together, I know you will never violate that, your character already dictates that, frankly, I'm some what taken back that God has placed you in my life"

Frankly, I was shocked she was in my life too.

After several hours in the park, I took her to some local pizza joint (her pick) then after that we went back to her apartment and played the card game "Phase 10" (I won) and that was our first date.

But when she hugged me goodbye, I honestly left numb, because I couldn't explain what happened to anyone. Because it didn't make sense to me. I had just spent the whole day with my female doppelganger. I was still kind of stunned.

When I got home, I lay in bed that night talking to God, asking him what had really happened today? Is this what it's like to have a woman finally really like me, without playing any games?

The day before I met Elisha, I had sat down with my closest guy friends and we had discussed my love for Lauren, and that I didn't know how I would ever get past her. But more so, with all these bad dates and relationships I'd had, Lauren had been the only one that showed signs of a potentially healthy relationship. So why didn't she want that? Better yet, want me? What did that say about me? Most of all, why would God, once again, give me someone to love and then just take her away?

That night, I lay awake wondering, was that about to happen again with Elisha?

Two days later she came to Lincoln because she hated central Nebraska. Upon receiving a brief tour of my town, she proclaimed, "Oh wow! There is so much to do here as opposed to the sinkhole I live in!"

That night I took her to dinner at my friend's restaurant as well this art walk event; we even snuck onto the field at Memorial Stadium (which, if you aren't from Nebraska, than you won't understand, but that is a big deal). We got ice cream and on the way there, we bumped into a pastor-friend of mine who has known me for years, and we conversed and he suddenly blurted out, "Wait… are you two on a date?"

"Yeah," I said. He grinned, and then said, "Well, then I'm totally going to embarrass Ryan and say Elisha, you really need to give this guy a chance. He is a keeper!" She interrupted him and said, "Oh, I know, he is one of the good guys, and there aren't many of those left." She smiled up at me. "I feel blessed to have him in my life already!"

I was pretty much speechless. This was so effortless. It was all clicking and happening so fast!

To end the night, Elisha pretty much blew me out of the water. Few women like *Star Wars*, but she did. We had this discussion on our first date about all it's merits and societal impact on culture—total "geek speak". Well, my close male friends and I play this board game called "Star Wars Epic Duels." If you have never played it, think "Dungeons & Dragons" but over simplified and equally as nerdy. Anyway, I told her about this on our first date, and she said that she wanted to play it, so that was how we ended the night: we went back to my house and played.

This made waves. When my male friends heard that a woman, by choice, played "Duels" (as we call it) on a date mind you, they were all speechless. Even my female friends couldn't fathom this. I can't quite explain how geeky this game is. But she loved it! She even asked if it would be okay to play with my friends, knowing she would be the only female there… I mean really, how can you not be impressed with her?

A couple of days later came Date #3. I offered to return to central Nebraska, but she said "No, all dates from now on will take place in Lincoln. Way more to do and I don't mind the drive because I'm getting to be with you!"

It was a Sunday, so I took her to church and she liked mine a ton. After church I took her to a farmer's market and then to lunch at Chipotle. She loved Chipotle--my favorite fast food place on the planet, then after that we went to the grocery store and bought groceries for a single mother and her disabled son who live in my neighborhood and who I help out on occasion. Elisha was taken aback when she realized that I was jobless and still buying groceries for someone else!

After that, I took her to a local lake, and we walked and talked. Just a great day together. At one point we had the most adult conversation ever, we sat down, and I told her that I desired to kiss her, but I didn't want to do that till she was ready. I enjoyed talking and connecting as much as we had but I didn't want to force anything. When she was ready for us to go down that road, I wanted to, but it was up to her. She told me that she wanted to as well, but this wasn't the right moment. Maybe later. It was all so casual and comfortable—like two adults talking matter-of-factly about their mutual attraction for each other. She told me we should go back to my house and watch *Donnie Darko* and snuggle on the couch. Now who wouldn't want that? Awesome woman and a flick? Yes please!

Nothing felt forced with her. In fact, she told me that day she wanted to go kayaking in a few days with me too, and suggested that we share a tent. She said she trusted me, because she knew that I wouldn't try going anywhere physically with her like other guys would. I was totally on board. With Elisha, I knew we could be in the same space and I wouldn't have to worry about sex, unlike Kelly, who was so eager to be with me, that I knew I'd have to be on my guard every second. I knew that Elisha and I were both committed to our boundaries, and I never feared that we would cross any lines. In fact, she started talking about vacations together and how we could get a hotel room together and she felt totally comfortable with that and even defending it to others, and I did to actually. We just had so much respect for each other.

Before our forth date, I sent her flowers. Little did I know that I was the first man to ever do that for her. In her 37 years of life, of all those that came before me, not one of them valued her that much. It was sad really because she is an amazing woman!

Date #4, she came to town and the plan was to go to the movies (she picked an action flick—YES!) and then dinner at my friend's burger joint. Finally, we would spend the rest of the night playing games with Paul and Melissa.

Before the movie, our first stop of the night, we were talking before the film started and Elisha told me something that kind of caught me off guard.

Before this date, she had told me about her family background, which was grim to say the least. Her mom was schizophrenic. Because of this, her dad left the family, running away with his secretary. He was gone for a few years and during that time, her mom got cancer and died. Several years later, she was eventually reunited with her father, who had now started a new life with his secretary. She also now had three half siblings and a "wicked step mother." Elisha couldn't even bear to say her name; she hated her that much. Turns out, her step mom would lock her in the basement and not feed her some days. Her father was in and out of the house on business trips frequently, so he wasn't there to put a stop to things. Elisha then shifted between that house and her grandparents, all this while her father was out of town on business. He never believed Elisha's cries for help, instead choosing his new wife over her. Her grandparents believed her and saw all this first hand on a few occasions, but they both died within a few years of each of other, so her teenage years were horrid.

But on that night's date, she added to this story.

She told me when she was younger, her mother frequently sexually assaulted her. She loved her mom and always spoke highly of her, previous to this discussion, and Elisha had come to a place of peace and comfort, that what happened to her was the work of her mother's mental illness. Elisha chose to only remember all the good and loving things her mother did, and treated the sexual abuse as merely a small stain in her past.

As a man, it was hard to not hurt for her. Having dated Annia and knowing that she experienced something very similar as Elisha, it only made me feel like now I was more prepared to be in a relationship with someone who had experienced that.

It helped too, because Elisha was solid in her relationship with God, when Annia had not been.

So her hesitation to have physical contact with me now made sense. It was going to be a process, just like with Annia, and I was ready to wait it out. Because after all, Elisha was moving to the West Coast in a few weeks, for a three month period and possibly longer. I was ready to go the distance, literally and figuratively for her. That's what I signed on for, and she told me the same. Despite her plans to leave, she wanted to continue to be in a relationship with me.

That night it rained, so that canceled my surprise star-watching in a park with chilled sparkling grape juice in champagne glasses (since neither of us drank). So we brought them to Paul and Melissa's. Elisha thought this was the cutest thing ever.

It was another great night together. Even better, Melissa got to meet her while our relationship was in its early stages and give her advice.

The next day Melissa, being a psychologist, called and told me that Elisha was the real deal. Her body language and the way she spoke to me, about me and with me indicated that Elisha was into me.

Then Date #5...

The whole day was weird.

That day started off with my first job interview in seventeen years. I had five weeks to prep for it—hey actually scheduled it that far out. With the interview on my mind, I was already nervous. But Elisha texted me that morning, encouraging me and telling me that I would do awesome, that she couldn't wait to spend the rest of the day with me, and regardless of the outcome, we had each other. Great! I thought.

Then I got another text...

Lauren broke her silence and wished me good luck as well. She'd heard through the grape vine that this was happening. She knew how hard I'd fought to get this interview and how at this point, I had worked endless side work type jobs to keep afloat. She'd previously told me how she admired my drive and my refusal to complain about my life circumstances, so hearing from the woman who, honestly, I still deeply loved, meant a lot.

Her text totally screwed with my mind, though.

It meant a lot, because I missed her obviously. But now, I was in a relationship with someone else...Elisha.

After the interview, I drove to central Nebraska where Elisha had a whole day planned for us. When I got there, we sat on her couch and she proclaimed, "First, we are going to go through this "Mad Libs" book." Oh man, now that screwed with my head even harder. I used to do that with Lauren! And Lauren just texted me that morning. I began to wonder, was this all some sort of sign?

I started to massage Elisha's shoulder and neck, and I asked for her permission to do so and she told me she really liked it. Her skin was smooth and her muscles were relaxed so I could tell she was comfortable with me touching her. She then put her hand on my knee and we kept "Mad-libbing" away. At one point, I thought she was about to kiss me, but instead she got up and poured us some sparkling grape juice she bought us with yes, champagne glasses. She was putting forth effort this time to please me, and I liked the cute little things she was doing.

She told me later in the night we were going to go for a walk and that we could massage each others feet. Sounds great, I thought. This spawned from a discussion about a foot massager she had on her floor that she got as a welcoming gift to her job, except it didn't work properly.

I also brought her a gift, a stuffed animal and set of books she mentioned that she was interested in reading one day. I wanted her to feel special—it's what I always strive for.

Not long after, she had a hair appointment. It was a mile away, so we walked. She was carrying a bag with her as well as her purse, so I offered to carry one of them. She said it wasn't necessary. And then I decided to just go for it: I asked if I could hold her hand. Strangely she said "no, but you can on the way home." I thought after having just received some knee touching action, that we were about to progress to the "hand holding phase"... but no.

After the appointment, we walked back to her place and there was no hand holding as promised. I was starting to become concerned.

We went back and played another game that was "question/answer" based; we continued to get to know each other on a deeper level and talked about a future together—the practicalities of that—and we were still in line with each other and our goals.

Despite the weirdness around the hand-holding, it was still a great day.

She made us dinner and it was fabulous. She was an awesome cook. In fact, she was the first woman that I have dated that ever made me dinner. Since I was the first to buy her flowers, I guess we took each others flower-giving and dinner-making virginities!

Later, we went to a park and walked, talked and laughed and while this was happening, I asked her "What dooms you in relationships? Since you said you never make it past date #5 and were on our fifth date and I'd like to obviously break that curse!

She said "Guys I have dated in the past, weren't good to me. But you are. So honestly, this is really a whole new experience for me to process."

Then I asked "Do you have a hard time expressing feelings and trusting guys then?"

She quickly responded with an exuberant "Oh, absolutely yes!"

Then, I pressed "Well, I'll be honest, I 'm not for sure if you like me, because we connected so well, but when you don't want to just snuggle, it just seems a bit strange to me. One second it seems you want to, then the next you don't, so are we ok?"

She tried to set me at ease when she said "I want to continue things, but I'm not sure I'm the one for you, because I'm moving and you want to stay in Nebraska."

I wasn't for sure at this point if she thought that since I was jobless that I would just move with her. Did she agree to get into a relationship with me because she thought if things worked out in our few weeks together, leaving with her would have been the next logical step for me?

After that, I wasn't sure where we stood. We went to a movie together and kept hanging out, we went back to her place and I gathered my things and left, but before I walked out the door… she gave me the semi-broken foot massager as a parting gift, I suppose.

The next day, I texted her, thanked her for the wonderful day and tried making future plans as always… but she wrote back and told be she wanted out and wanted to go to the West coast with no attachments. She said that she hated Nebraska and planned to never return. I was stunned. It all seemed so harsh and sudden. All these future plans we had—gone.

After that, I returned through the wormhole to my life before her.

Still no job, still the same family and friends, still wondering if Lauren would ever love me.

I think my experience with Elisha was God putting a quality woman in my world during a dark and confusing time for me. She was something I could focus on instead of dwelling on the uncertainty of my future ahead. I actually take comfort in that, especially since I never kissed her, but more so because I know I respected her in the way I treated her during our time together and that when we she meets someone else and they ask about the other men she's dated, she can at least throw me into the "good guy" category.

I also think our time together was a reminder from God that though I don't understand exactly why

Lauren may never love me, my efforts and the way I treat the women I date, doesn't go un-noticed. And maybe one day, one will actually stick around and want what I have to offer, forever.

Chapter 10
Ninja Date #2

At the time, I was working in medical records at a local hospital. There were about 150 people in our department, spread out over different shifts. So it was always tough to really get to know people.

Claire, however, was someone that I was chummy with. She was friendly, kinda of plain, obsessed with country music and small town life, since that is where she grew up; so we didn't always have a lot of talking points to connect on, and she just wasn't my type.

Needless to say, Claire invited me to a softball game; she said they needed a 2nd baseman and I agreed to go. I figured it was a great way to meet co-workers and finally put faces with the names of people I email everyday (this was pre-Facebook). Plus, I loved playing softball back in the day, so I was pumped to dust off my old glove and make a night of things.

My Friday night would be spent bonding with my co-workers over a baseball diamond.

Claire said to meet at a local restaurant; everyone was going gather there first to get drinks and appetizers before hand.

So I showed up to this restaurant that I had never been to; I assumed it was a sports bar, since again, we were all about to go play softball together and drinks and appetizers were broadcasted to be the main source of pre-game substance.

Now, I admit, I could have done a little research on the place before hand, but either way, I showed up to the restaurant in cleats, sweat pants meant for sliding in the dirt and a fairly standard white-trash-friendly shirt that you don't mind getting dirty in because it has 10 different shades of paint stains on it… however, this place had a dress code. I was now forced to put on a blazer jacket, and I was seated at a table with Claire and then two other co-workers I knew, Mitch and Raquel. No other co-workers were present, no one else that resembled anyone who was about to indulge in a softball game. I'd just arrived at a ninja date!

And it only got worse.

"Plain" Claire was wearing earrings, makeup and a dress, the first sign that this was headed in a non-softball direction.

But little did I know, I had stumbled onto something bigger…

Mitch and Raquel were holding hands, which was shocking because Mitch was married… to someone else!

Mitch was sort of a hero around work. He always shaved his head, in tribute to his wife because she lost all her hair as part of her ongoing battle with breast cancer. He would always wear some breast-cancer-awareness-oriented shirt at least once a week, so everyone knew how supposedly committed he was to his wife while she struggled with cancer.

So now I'd stumbled onto Mitch and Raquel's dirty secret and I felt super uncomfortable.

As I sat down, Raquel asked, "Did you just come from a softball game?"

"No," I said, unwilling to embarrass Claire (although part of me wanted to). "I was, uh, hoping to play in one tonight and just thought I would come prepared for a pick up game".

Mitch and Raquel obviously had no idea what Claire was up to. If they did, they did a good job of hiding it. Either way, I looked stupid in what I was wearing. I looked like a hodgepodge of athletic chic. Actually, I looked like something out of that scene from *Major League* when Charlie Sheen is forced to go to that upscale restaurant to help Tom Berenger win back Rene Russo.

When dinner was done, I split.

The weekend passed and Monday at work, I crossed paths with Melinda, who I knew was pals with Raquel. Melinda and I were friends around the office, and at the water cooler, she asked about my weekend. I told her all about my ninja date on Friday night, and she told me she knew already about the affair and that she had been begging Raquel to end it.

Then the kicker (pun intended)… she went on to tell me a story she'd heard, that Mitch, when he was 16, along with three friends, killed an immigrant, cut off his head and together they played soccer with it. He served a light sentence since he was a minor at the time of the crime and was part of a group that collectively killed someone and because he was deemed insane at the time as well.

This sounded pretty far fetched… but then again, it made me wonder what else was he hiding. He lied to each of us everyday at work about his love for his cancer-stricken wife, all the while banging Raquel on the side.

Mitch and I had always been cool around the office. I had always thought he was a nice guy. But now I couldn't look at him the same way.

Part of me was curious as to what this said about me. Because of his friendship with Claire and Raquel, he knew there was a chance I might show up that night and bear witness to his adultery. So did he think I would be cool with it and non-judgmental or something to that effect?

Either way, later that day when I passed Mitch in the halls, I just said hi like normal, but it felt awkward.

Shortly after this, Claire got a job elsewhere and so did Mitch. He moved out of state and Raquel followed him!

Awkward!

Chapter 11
Who am I Dating Here? You? You? or You? and Other Blonde Adventures

I have this curse… I never get to date blondes. Not even women with hair dyed blonde. If you hair color is blonde, for some reason the color communicates telepathically to the women "don't date Ryan".

I like all hair colors and styles in general. But I tend to gravitate toward brunettes, or they are the only ones that say yes, I'm not sure.

Somehow though, after years of attempts, I actually got a blonde to agree to go out with me. This however, didn't come without pleading. My date with "Kendra" took some major convincing!

I messaged her on a dating site… no response (typical). But she checked out my profile. Then a week later, she checked out my profile again and I sent her another message. No response. Bored and not ready to throw in the towel, a week later I sent one final message… this time however, she finally took the time to view my profile thoroughly I guess and subsequently emailed me and said she'd like to meet up that weekend.

I was pumped. A blonde is finally going out with me… and a cute one at that!

My original plan was to take her to the comedy club, then sushi and drinks after.

She opted for just the sushi and drinks.

So I had to wait 5 days before we could go out. Each day that week, something strange happened, she kept viewing my dating profile… so why is this strange you might ask? Because I felt, she read my profile, my details and gave my mug a good look over, then she obviously approved of me via our online conversation, enough that she agreed to go out… so why is it every day since, she was looking at my profile still?

Part of me thought… no big deal, she is probably continuing her research on me and by the time we link up, she is going to have a barrage of questions for me, she'll put me through the "Spanish inquisition" and we'll have fun. My profile gave her tons of info on me, tons of possible expansion questions could come from it.

The pessimist part of me thought, maybe she is looking everyday because she is having second thoughts and is trying to convince herself to show up and give me a chance?

So the big night arrives, an hour before hand, she tell me she is bringing her friend Tori… she says that Tori just got out of the hospital 2 days ago and had a rib removed and needs some cheering up… now I'm not thrilled that now I have to impress two girls and not just one. But when I arrive, Kendra and Tori bring there friend Hailey! That's right, now there are three girls.

The best case scenario of the "Spanish Inquisition" at the hands of Kendra now just turned into a firing squad at the assistance of her pals!

Bringing 2 friends as back up, just to get past the gates to get to have conversation with Kendra?

Really? What is she, "Regina George" from *Mean Girls*?

Then the kicker…

So Hailey looked really familiar… and I never forget a face! And I was right, she had been checking out my dating profile all month too… so who was I here to date? Kendra or Hailey? Did Kendra just say "yes" to help out Hailey in meeting me? If Kendra wasn't a real person, I would have thought I was being "Catfished" or something!

Hailey did all the talking that night too (she was a brunette by the way).

But the funny thing was, Tori was being really flirty and engaging in this conversation with me too.

So I asked Tori (also a brunette) about this rib removal thing. I was curious if she was in a car accident or something… all she would say was she had it removed for "medical reasons". I asked if she had an extra rib or something and she said no, just that again, she had to have a rib removed for medical reasons… I thought that was kind of sketchy, but whatever.

After a few martinis, later in the night, Tori still wouldn't spill the beans on the rib. Call me nosey, but don't you too want to know why a perfectly healthy, beautiful woman is randomly getting her lower rib removed? I heard that some women do it to attempt to get a smaller waist line… as best as I could figure, that might be why she did it? Tori would have looked hot still though, even with the extra rib if that was the case.

I mean really, who gets a single rib removed? Don't you find this intriguing? I kept hearing the voice of Chris Rock in *I'm Gonna Get You Sucka* saying "How much for just one rib!".

If you get a single rib removed, do they give it to you in a jar of formaldehyde when all is said and done?

Frankly, the quest to find the fate of the rib was the most interesting part of the date…

Because Kendra wasn't talking at all!

No seriously, for a gal who viewed my profile all week, she had virtually no questions for me, Tori and Hailey steered the conversation all night. Kendra just seemed disinterested.

On her wrists she had tattoos. One was of a cross and I thought, ok cool. She's claims to be a Christian, has an overtly Christian tattoo on her wrist, so I asked her about that and she said "I used to believe, but don't actively practice now. Kind of like Katy Perry, her faith is her roots, but she is having too much fun straying away right now, she enjoys the moral concepts and still incorporates some of them in her life today, I'm much of the same."

When a girl quotes a pop star instead of a pastor, you know you're doomed.

I ask her how long she had been single and she said 2 weeks. She was living with some guy for a year and he had 3 kids and it was just too much to handle, so she bailed… so at this point I realized I was a rebound at best. Kendra was not looking for a potential relationship like me and like her profile claimed she was, she was just looking for attention of some kind.

I kept chatting with Hailey and Tori while Kendra fiddled on her phone!

Eventually, I joked about Kendra being bored and constantly on her phone and then I bluntly said "Hailey, that text you just got, was that from Kendra telling you to make an excuse so you all can leave?" and Hailey busted out laughing and Kendra's face went bright red!

And no sooner did I say that then Tori and Hailey were gone; oh yeah and Kendra too, you know, the girl I was supposed to be on a date with?

The blonde streak continued and ended a couple of weeks later…

I went out with another blonde, her name was "Amy"…

Not much to tell except it was one of the most awkward endings to a date yet.

Amy was super fun. She had that "one of the guys" type of personality, probably because of her military background, super cute too.

We sat for 2 hours and had dinner and drinks. We had a ton of laughs and liked a lot of the same things and she was a "Rollergirl" to boot! Those Rollergirls, they're a different breed in themselves, they are sassy, dangerous and fun!

After 2 hours of connecting, somehow the subject of sex came up. I told her I was a virgin and she said she wasn't. She then asked me more about that, I told her that I was trying to follow God's plan for all of us and no sooner did I say that, than she asked for the check! I asked her if I said anything wrong and she said no, but she said honestly that she feels that she wants a relationship and that she has to "sample before she buys" and she knew that I wouldn't conform to that and cut ties right then and there... It was a bummer in a way, because we connected on many other things, but sex was the deal breaker again and then she was gone. I never dated a blonde since.

Ironically, I checked in with Amy a few weeks after our date, she got engaged and married some dude in a span of 3 months... I guess she liked what I can only assume she sampled before she bought. She did however tell me that the way I live my life inspired her to be more diligent in her faith and inspired her to seek it more, but just not regarding that one issue that divided us.

The End?

As I end this, I hope you had a laugh and maybe a cry as well. Maybe you related to some of my misadventures, maybe you've had some of your own that top mine? (I sure hope so!)

Either way, my story isn't too dissimilar to many of yours. We all struggle when we are single, constantly asking ourselves, why is this happening? Is it us? Or is it them? What do I need to do differently?

"What do I need to do differently?" I really want to challenge that question, with this:

You can change your appearance, your interests, whatever, but, does that make you... you? If you love *Star Wars*... then own it! You just might find someone who loves it as much as you and meet that special someone, but you might also make some awesome friends along the way too, people that might not only love *Star Wars*, but are in the same life position as you and now you'll have someone to commiserate with or hopefully encourage you in your singlehood.

People say, "The moment you stop looking is when it happens." Personally I disagree. Keep looking—you never know who might be looking as well. If you like someone, don't play games; just go for it!

However, I want to encourage my fellow single folk out there with this:

Many of you will not be getting married, possibly me included.

Sorry, I hate to be the one who bears bad news, but it's a sad reality in some ways.

Some words that I often meditate on are from a pastor out of NYC named Timothy Keller. He said this:

"If you say 'I trusted God to come through for me and he didn't' than you only trusted Him to meet your agenda."

I love that.

I think one of most abused passages in the bible is Psalm 37:4. "Take delight in the Lord, and he will give you the desires of your heart." I agree with the first part… we should love the Lord… but the after effect of that will not result in a house, car, romantic relationship, or whatever you "desire." I'm not going against God here, all I'm saying is I feel that many preachers use this out of context and instead tell people that God will "reward" them for a lack of better terms for following Him. More accurately, I think it should say that God will "provide" for you. When you follow Him, and I've seen it time and time again, somehow all I really need to survive is provided for me by Him! He is the "great sustainer" after all.

I think some of the churches I've attended through the years have lied to me, to us, with regards to that Psalm passage. God is not a slot machine—what you put into Him, you shouldn't expect that and more in return. The reality is, he sent his Son to die on a cross for us; that gift is enough and we should be grateful for that ALONE!

If you think that God owes you ANYTHING… then prepared to be disappointed.

I don't know if you have seen *Bruce Almighty*, but there is a scene in it that is brilliant. When Bruce gets God's powers for a day and answers everyone's prayers all at once and the world collapses basically, because that is what life is... God has to say "no" to things, to some of our "desires", no matter how much we wanted them, because He knows that us getting what we desired, at the time we wanted it in some cases, would have ultimately wrecked us. That's why we didn't get it in the first place. As he says in his Word in 1st Peter 5:7, "Let Him have all your worries and cares, for He is always thinking about you and watching everything that concerns you" or as the saying goes "God wrecks your plans before they wreck you!" So in those moments that we didn't get what we desired, we have to remember that He has a bigger purpose, as hard as it is for us to accept.

I know, trust me, that's hard to accept. Especially try telling that to a person who lost a child, or has been diagnosed with a terminal disease or is suffocating from whatever emotional ill that is consuming them; how do you tell them that loss is a blessing from God? Though true, it's tough.

Another movie scene that I think is prolific is from *The Exorcism of Emily Rose*, when Emily is demon-possessed and near death, she sees the Virgin Mary and she offers her the option to die peacefully NOW or to continue to endure the pain that her demon-possessed body is consumed by and die a horrible death, but He will make an example of her death for His glory! That is a tough pill to swallow... but I think that is also what life is all about!

Life is about pushing forward for His glory, no matter how disillusioned we may get at times.

Look at Jesus for a moment, though he was a carpenter by trade, no one remembers Him for the oak cabinets he made back then, but instead for the things he did with his life! Jesus was single, and in that singlehood he led an extremely significant life and if you are single, you too should strive to live a life that is equally significant!

As much as I wanted to be an entertainer or a husband or a father… God is clearly saying those things are not in the cards for me, not now still and possibly forever. The Hell I create for myself is when I'm constantly fighting against the tide, trying to prove Him wrong, which constantly leads to more and stronger heartaches each time, even though he warned me! Look at the Bible: it's story after story of people trying to go their own way, not listening to Him, and then wrecking themselves. God is still there, waiting to pick up the pieces for them, even after their selfishness and defiance. The same is true today of us as well.

So in a strange way, I am kind of like Emily Rose, despite not getting what I want, or what I think is right for me, I endure. I keep waking up each day and asking, "What's next for me God"?

I can't say my life has been a waste, because it hasn't. When I look at all my volunteer work and my missions or humanitarian work, I never saw half of that coming, but God constantly threw that on my lap and said, "Do this." In that, I have inspired others to follow my lead.

We are all significant people in our own way; it may not be in the way we wanted or expected, but it's in the way God wanted for us to best glorify Him, so don't sell yourself short or let anyone tell you different!

"God is not concerned with our happiness, he is concerned with us being fulfilled with Him alone."
-Ravi Zacharias

Credits:

I would like to thank, acknowledge or apologize to the following people for playing a role in my life and for being a part of it so far:

To my Lord and savior Jesus Christ for dying on a cross on my behalf and being there for me when no one else is! But most importantly, for giving me the gift of eternal life, for which I am beyond unworthy of.

My Mom and Dad (LaRee and Joe), for providing and caring for me through all these years and for tolerating my act. You deserve a whole page worth of "thank you's" so I hope you can just accept this simple statement… thank you for endless sacrifices and for all that you have done for me.

My birth mom Becky for choosing life.

Mark and Ashley Hustad and family, for their constant friendship and support.

A very special thanks to Mark for not just being my best friend, but for being the brother I never got to have. I've known you half my life now and shared some of my greatest memories and experiences with you, I'm so thankful God blessed me with a friend as faithful as you. From playing video games till 4 a.m. to crazy vacations, I'm lucky to have been able to share it all with you. Also, behind the scenes, for helping me come up with the cover art design, designing the website and gathering most of the information that led to this book's publishing. Thanks again Mark… for everything!

Thanks to the entire Hustad clan while we're at it, for putting up with me for all these years.

Nat and Tiffany Crawford and family, for their constant friendship and support.

A very special thanks to Nat as well for being my other best friend, my other "brother from another mother", for the years of friendship, adventures and general stupid stuff we have done together, for a life time of laughs and for believing in me. God has been too generous to me to put you in my life. Through all the hardships, you've always been a constant in my life and faithful friend. I love you bro!

Lucas and Meredith Megrue for you guessed it, their constant friendship and support.

A very special thanks to Lucas also, for constantly believing in me and helping me develop into the man of God I am and still trying to become. Thanks for the hours of heated "Duels" games as well. Pitch tournaments and Husker games. We've had a lot of fun together. Thanks bro!

Mike and Kristin Sukraw, for the prayer and advice that has lasted me a lifetime! Thanks for caring! Thanks Mike for your friendship and for the Godly example you have set for me to follow, both in marriage and in life.

A very special thanks to Kristin for being my "dating coach" and for the suggestions for this book. Truthfully, your help and praise deserves more than a sentence! Thanks for all your time and kindness. "Funstad" appreciates it!

Mike and Rachel Schlabz and family, for all the love and laughs.

The entire Jablonski family as well.

Eric and Amanda Kasik and family for their constant friendship and support

David and Terri Travis and family for their constant friendship and support and for the many great nights of laughs, serious talks and card games.

Stacy Anderson for her years of friendship, advice and support.

An extremely special thanks to Andrew Hustad and Lucas Megrue for constantly building me up, enjoying my writing through the years and for encouraging and pushing me to do this book.

Amanda Snider, for being the first to read this book, actually believing what I had to say had value and merit… and to think, one of these chapters could have been about you! But you'd rather move to China and get away from me… I can't blame you! But you saying that my writing reminded you of "Donald Miller" is really what kept driving me to keep going, because he is a successful writer and if I can somehow be even a fraction as successful as him, then I'm all for it. So thanks for your encouragement.

Thanks to Lindsay Morgan Snyder and her constructive criticism that also helped shape this book at the 11th hour. You can check out her writing at Puttingthepencildown.com

To the women featured in this book known as Annia, Jamie, Kelly, Lauren and Elisha, thank you for allowing me to be a part of your life… you may regret that now, but you will always have a special place in my heart. Just know what I wrote was not intended to be done or said in malice.

Dani Dornbusch… for being all that you are.

A special thanks to the greatest band I ever got to play in and be a part of, "Waiting for Gabe" with my friends Ben Harms, Erik Hustad, Mark Hustad, Chris Lawson, Gabe Lovelace. Thanks for the years worth of memories and being a large reason why I'm still single. Thanks for helping me miss out on my prime dating years. I actually don't regret that… well, maybe.

Pastors Bryan Clark, Dan Lehman and Matt Meyer and Lincoln Berean Church for helping me to stay centered and in check.

Thanks to my family at KIBZ 1041 The Blaze, for the years of laughs at a time in my life when I needed them, especially the morning crew and for giving me the many opportunities I might not have otherwise ever had.

The deepest of thanks to my editor Liz Eberspacher, for editing my atrocious grammar and for challenging, encouraging and making me a better writer. This book is better because of you. Thanks for helping me look less stupid! Thanks to Clint as well for being my friend and his Godly insight in my life.

Pastor Ron Drury, thanks for being my other editor, but more so for the years of friendship, prayer, encouragement and for supporting all my bands through the years as well.

Thanks to John Kimmel Creative for designing such an awesome cover and layout for this book! Contact him at: jkimmelcreative@gmail.com

Thanks to Jennie Prescott for the amazing headshots for this book and Carl Prescott and the Prescott family for always being there to help with the countless computer issues I had to endure while writing this.

Timothy Benavidez for his years of friendship.

A very special thanks to Mark Salomon, his book *Simplicity* touched me and helped me through a dark period in my life. The honesty in his words about his life inspired me in part to write the way I did about mine in this book. Plus, his band Stavesacre has always been an encouragement to me and has inspired me as a musician as well. I can't begin to say thank you enough to you.

... and finally to YOU for actually buying and reading this! Thanks for your support!

For all personal inquires and questions for the author, please feel free to contact him at:
notquitelovebook@gmail.com or
http://www.notquitelove.com